G000059838

DOMINIC HOLLAND

VOL.2

Acknowledgments

I am always grateful to my good friend Marcus Landau of Conker Design for yet another book cover.

My thanks to Andrea Coates and Mike Stallard, my two proofreaders. Two friends who are much cleverer than me. Their time has been invaluable but also somewhat costly because it is probable that I will now forfeit two book sales and believe me, they all count.

Nikki was the earliest reader of these *Takes*, whittling things down from about fifty essays to the final thirty-one. If there are no *Takes* you enjoy in this volume, then spare a thought for my poor wife.

Other notable readers and editorial guides to thank and in order… Sam Holland, Tom Holland and then finally, Harry Holland. I didn't ask Paddy and he didn't offer.

Ryan Ashcroft of *Book Brand* for designing, putting the book together and for his unerring knack for spotting errant typos.

Morna Walters of *Puzzle Communications* for her considerable help against the ongoing IT conspiracy that is being waged against me.

To my man, Raef Meeuwisse who advises me in on all things independent publishing. A man who is severely put upon and would do well to learn the word, no.

And finally, to the kind people on my Patreon who have remained with me since lockdown and have both encouraged this new volume and offered encouraging feedback on early *Takes*.

Prologue

Welcome to my second volume of *Takes on Life*, a series of books written with worthy intentions. A collection of comic essays exposing my quirks, shortcomings and foibles which I hope will chime with readers.

Back when my boys were very young, I had a line in my stand-up act which went something like this…

"…I travel the country making people laugh. It's an odd job but someone's got to do it. But it's confusing for my little boys. Because they know their dad makes people laugh for a living, but they're embarrassed by this because they think I go around the country tickling people…"

I do far fewer gigs these days, so I am fortunate to have my writing as an outlet. Laughter is said to be good for the soul and since laughter is my business, you should expect some funny moments in the pages ahead. That said, creating laughs on stage is much easier than from the page. I don't know why I point this out. Maybe because this book is searingly honest or perhaps I am covering myself in the event that laughs are scant.

You might be aware that an integral element of successful comedy is timing. It has been said that *Takes on Life* is an ideal gift and advisable therefore to publish in time for Christmas. Publishing after Christmas then is poor timing and does not augur well.

I should also explain that not all *Takes* are funny. Some are poignant and written to provoke thoughts and reflection. It should be apparent which is which. If this is not the case then I have got things wrong and I offer my apologies in advance.

That there are thirty-one *Takes* is no accident. This book is meant to be read whilst sitting in the smallest room in the house and I hope that for even the longest month of the year, it can replace the phones we are so beholden to. Bowel movements are good for us, but so is reading.

Books are good for our brains and our mental health, but reading is a skill we are losing to technology and a world where it seems that everything requires a plug.

This is why *Takes on Life* is short and easy to read. *Less is more*, as the adage goes, which each *Take* strictly adheres to. Economically written to maximise their impact and make a compelling book which readers will wish to share with everyone they care about and to publicise on all their social media channels!

Hmm…

This is a bold claim and might be a terrible overreach. It certainly heaps pressure on the opening *Take* – appropriately called *Less is More* and attempts to demonstrate this message literally and metaphorically.

Thank you for coming to this book. Whatever your reasoning, I hope it serves a purpose. I have enjoyed writing it enormously, but of course, this is not enough. I enjoy playing golf but no one would pay to watch me play.

As already flagged, the intention of *Takes on Life* is a simple one; to make readers feel good. A noble goal. I hope it works.

Take One

Less is More

An intrinsic value of gold is its scarcity and this typifies the adage, *Less is More*, which is sage advice and applicable to so many areas of life.

It certainly applies prominently in the arts. The days of the taut ninety-minute movie are long gone, replaced with unwieldy epics in desperate need of an edit. I didn't catch Scorsese's *The Irishman* because I couldn't risk devoting three hours of my finite life to something I might not sufficiently enjoy.

But the best demonstration of *Less is More* is found in the opaque world of beauty.

In my entire adulthood, I estimate that I have spent less than £50 on my skin and this includes shaving foam which I stopped using once I realised that a sharp razor blade does not need any assistance to cut hair. I did once buy a bottle of Nivea aftershave balm which I still have somewhere in the house, although not to hand.

In contrast, my wife Nikki, has fully embraced skin care and is completely on-board with the dubious promises and claims made by people wearing white coats and spectacles.

And with skin lotions and potions, it appears that less is most definitely more. More money, anyway. Much more money. In fact, the price of a skin lotion seems inversely proportional to the amount of cream. The smaller the amount, the higher the price.

And here's the real kicker…

The more expensive a cream, apparently, the greater its effectiveness.

The universal law of economies of scale is turned upside down by cosmetics. Customers do not want skin cream in bulk. Big tubs of lotion with a plunge dispenser have no place in the world that promises age reversal.

Instead, these magical creams are presented in thimble sized jars. Tiny tubs of wizardry within large and reassuringly expensive packaging.

Welcome to the alchemy of turning false promises into gold.

The cosmetics industry enjoys a unique and enviable sales proposition…

Namely, the more expensive a product, the better it is perceived to work and the smaller amount of product on offer, the more customers must have it and the more they are willing to pay.

And these customers are remarkably committed to this cause. So loyal that they continue to buy said expensive creams even though they age at exactly the same rate as everyone else.

Back in the day, I regularly appeared on television and was a 'celebrity' of the lower leagues. My 'stardom' has faltered now but with my large social media following, perhaps I have a second chance.

A caveat here...

A vicarious following (I know) based almost entirely on a certain famous member of my family.

But no matter. My metrics are my own, however they are acquired and I note that 'influencers' are doing very nicely indeed.

Any mention of a brand nowadays can make healthy returns, at least with free stuff, if not cold hard cash.

More cunning readers might have spotted already my mention of *Nivea* and might suspect a pecuniary motive and on this, allow me to exonerate myself. I have not mentioned this world brand (twice already) and about to be three (*Nivea*) to curry favour and garner free wares because I don't need anything that *Nivea* (four) has to offer.

Because however many years I have left, my current tub of *Nivea* (five) will see me out and will be duly handed down to my four boys to share between them.

And if they're anything like me, they will have plenty to go around.

Take Two

Ignorance is Not Always Bliss

I am mindful that this book is not a series of embarrassing anecdotes but some instances are just too good not to share...

Having completed my public exams in 1985 (O-levels), I spent the summer in Ireland with my cousins. A holiday for me and a break for my parents. And what a holiday it was for a sixteen year old. I fell in love for the first time with a beautiful Irish girl called Mary. Our fledgling courtship blossomed quickly (for me at least) until I contracted a mouth infection and was confined to bed for weeks on end with hundreds of ulcers.

I stopped eating and lost weight rapidly with hushed talk around my bedside about what might have caused such a violent infection. Swimming in the River Shannon came high on the list and I was relieved that no one mentioned my heavy petting (snogging) with Ireland's most beautiful sixteen year old as a possible cause. Oral thrush was mentioned which I registered but didn't understand and I thought little of it as the ulcers eventually cleared. I returned home a little more worldly-wise (manly?) albeit half the weight and I never saw Mary again.

Back to school for my two senior years, my summer of love behind me although a nagging doubt remained about my health and what might have caused the infection. In a history class, Mr Dacey lost his patience with me and suggested I should sit closer to the front or else get my eyes tested – which is important for this story and chain of events.

I had chosen to do biology as one of my three subjects for A-level. The easiest of the sciences but also because biology was taught at a local all-girls school, my hope being that I might learn biology more in the practical sense than just the theory.

My impaired vision was confirmed by an optometrist and my joy at finally seeing clearly for the first time was impinged by my health anxiety and specifically my sexual health.

In essence, I was worried that I had contracted a venereal disease (VD) after my summer of unconsummated love.

For this diagnosis I did not have much to go on. Mainly anecdotal evidence from other boys who like me, knew bugger all. I had gleaned some information about Herpes. Mainly that it cannot be cured or eradicated and if untreated it can lead to something called Syphilis.

My mum was a nurse and would have been a good reference point until I factored in she was also a very Catholic nurse, so I was left to research things for myself which unsurprisingly turned out to be a disaster.

Pre-internet of course, all I had to go on were my dad's heavy and dusty encyclopaedias. Probably six months on from my Irish dalliance but still fretting, I finally plucked up the courage to find the volume for all things beginning with S.

Sambuca, Sicily, sombreros, sport, sugar and something else...

oh yes, Syphilis.

I read with trepidation, my finger quivering and my breath quickening. Initially, my worries abated because I did not have the symptoms described. My penis was not burning and it did not have a painful discharge. The relief was enormous. I should have stopped reading then and got on with my young manhood but I didn't. I read on and my world collapsed…

I'm paraphrasing here but the text went something like this…

…the disease can lie dormant in the body for a considerable time with no symptoms presenting. The disease affects internal organs including the brain. It can impair vision, even leading to blindness and can eventually cause death…

Immediately my vision blurred (not helpful) as my mind scrambled back to that history lesson with Mr Dacey.

"Holland, you need glasses."

Now I understood why. My three siblings all had perfect vision. Yes, because they haven't got a deadly disease.

And who could I turn to?

No one.

I was on my own which brings me to my biology classes – at the local girls school – which just so happened to be directly opposite a sexual diseases clinic.

Not ideal, clearly.

Much better to attend a clinic where no one will recognise me and especially not the girls in my bloody class. How attractive will they find me if they think I am diseased?

But not knowing how long I had left to live, or at least before I went blind, I was desperate and had no other option.

I didn't wear a disguise but I did take off my school tie and I might have hitched up the lapel of my jacket as I shot through the doors of the clinic. Disorientated and panicked I made little sense to the receptionist who must have been surprised to have such a young patient.

The waiting room was awkward. Lots of wizened-looking adults and one child.

I had an initial consultation with a nurse which was not straightforward as I explained my unusual circumstances. My summer, the ulcers and you know, going blind. Although, I still had sufficient vision to catch her wry smile at the child before her.

She probably could have dismissed me then but maybe protocols prevented her. It's hazy now what happened and when. I think a blood test was taken. But I definitely recall a swab being taken from inside my penis – something I will never forget.

And then I had to wait to see the doctor.

In my mind, this consultation took place on the same day although it might have been days/weeks later when the results came back.

But I do recall meeting with a handsome male doctor and shaking with fear.

Doc, man to man, just tell me straight. How long have I got?

He read my notes with some obvious confusion and I noted again that same affectionate smile. But then he hit me with a question that was even more painful than the internal examination of my urethra.

"…when did you last have sexual intercourse?"

I could have lied of course but for the small matter of my life being on the line. Now was the time for complete candour and to hell with any embarrassment.

"Erm, I haven't. Well, not yet anyway…"

His smile increased.

"…I mean, I could have done." I went on, limply. "Just that, you know, I didn't want to be irresponsible…"

By passing on a deadly plague that I might be incubating.

He almost chuckled now. A little ray of sunshine perhaps in an otherwise difficult day seeing patients with noxious discharges and no doubt other social problems also.

He shared the good news with me.

That I was in perfect health albeit a little short-sighted.

I thanked him profusely. I nearly went in for a hug.

And on my way out of his office, he left me with words I will never forget…

"Go get 'em tiger."

Take Three

A Hero Amongst Us

The health benefits of dog ownership are legion. Their companionship alone is invaluable. Their loyalty and affection is unrelenting and heartening. Dogs are dependable and consistent. Dogs can be cuddled. They are warm. They need to be walked, thereby the owner is bound to exercise and will reap enormous health upsides. Our dog, Tessa, is eight years old and I calculate that conservatively I have walked 3,640 miles that I would not have walked without her. A heart benefit which cannot be claimed by any of the four Holland boys, by the way.

Oxygen and water might head up the essentials for life on Earth but love is not far behind. It is crucial that we love something and that we too, feel loved.

I coined the following adage for the Holland household...

*Tessa is the only Holland who is loved by everyone **all** of the time.*

She is unassailably the most popular member of our family and we all vie for her affection and compete to be her favourite human.

Which happens to be me and which I can prove by recounting an incident when Nikki and I were on a dog walk in Richmond Park, London's biggest open space.

On the walk, we encountered a dog walker with two Staffordshire Bull Terriers (Staffies in the UK, Pit Bulls in the US). He assured us his dogs were friendly until one of them pinned Tessa to the ground and began biting lumps out of her. Overwhelmed by a dog with its jaw clamped to her thigh while its owner did nothing, Nikki was unable to even look and was no use whatsoever. But nevertheless, thank goodness she was present and more on this later, when all will become clear.

Fortunately for Tessa though, an intrepid hero was on hand.

Me.

Without any thought for my own safety, I entered the melee against a breed of dog famed for its jaw which can only be released by thrusting a red-hot poker up its arse.

Without such a weapon to hand, I prised open its jaw to free my beloved dog. To be fair, the dog gave up fairly easily but I couldn't have known this at the time and I haven't shared this information with anyone until now. Finally released, Tessa made a beeline for Nikki who was now standing at a safe distance, about thirty feet away and in floods of tears.

And thank goodness that the dog didn't turn on me. His owner was able to reattach its lead whereupon we had a frank exchange about what constituted friendliness.

Like our dogs, we were never destined to become friends and we quickly moved off in a different direction, both literally and metaphorically. If he ever comes by this book, I wonder if he might recognise himself but I suspect not. I don't have him down as much of a reader.

Nikki and I were both badly shaken but in less pain than Tessa with her badly punctured leg. She would need medical attention but my wounds began to heal immediately. Firstly, in the knowledge that I had saved my dog's life and secondly because she knew who had rescued her.

But from here, an unexpected upside emerged with increased admiration and affection from the other notable female in my life. Immediately I began to revel in my newly found hero status.

Nothing I have accomplished to date, either on stage or in my writing has ever made Nikki so impressed with the man she settled for.

"Dom, you were so brave…"

Oh, really… No, but do go on…

"No, seriously, Dom. What would I have done if you hadn't been with me?"

A metaphor for our life together, surely, but I managed to keep this thought to myself.

The young vet was also sympathetic. She already knew Tessa, having assisted with her emergency operation after she was gored by a stag in the same park. A brilliant young woman, she asked all the right questions…

"And how did you get the attacking dog to release its jaw?"

Well…

Our little dog was stitched, patched and jabbed with various needles before she was good-to-go. And it must be said without a jot of gratitude, even as I paid the £280 bill.

Not that I needed her thanks of course. She has been a godsend for the Holland family and has a huge credit balance.

Plus, I am enjoying my boosted self-esteem, fanned by Nikki sharing the story of her valiant husband with everyone she meets. Our boys included, who now understand that their old man is not just a clown. There is more than one hero in the Holland household and one of them does not require a special suit.

Take Four

Where Were You When...

A successful marriage is a product of many things but most importantly, enough common ground and compatibility.

Children are common ground. Houses might be the largest purchase we ever make but no matter how painful, whilst possessions can be liquidated and distributed, children are a constant. We are parents forever and children are a useful glue.

Our four boys are the fruits of our marriage and because my becoming a dad (now an old man) is my most important achievement, I am mindful to preserve the thing that allowed this to happen. Sure, we needn't have got married. The majority of couples don't bother these days, but I believe that marriage is a factor in couples staying together. Or sticking it out?

Not that kids are enough to sustain every marriage. Staying together for the children is often cited but sometimes this is not the case and who am I to judge?

And I am not implying that staying married has been some kind of burden or sacrifice for me and brings me to the nub of this *Take*.

Compatibility.

Being compatible is crucial and particularly so since physical attraction is bound to wane.

Couples that think similarly and agree on the bigger issues can expect more yards than the ones at loggerheads.

I have an example of our compatibility which I venture might account for our success (so far) and why we are better off together than apart.

We are all familiar with… *I remember what I was doing, when*… and then complete with your own seismic event: 9/11, the death of Princess Diana or Queen Elizabeth II, JFK, England winning any major sports trophy…

When we first got married, we spent a lot of time in a beautiful part of North East England called Northumberland. A friend from university had a family cottage in a coastal town called Bamburgh. An expansive sandy beach complete with a stunning castle, it is one of the great seascapes of Britain and is frequently used as a backdrop in movies.

In 1996 and first-time parents to a boy who never slept, together with our friends (and their newborn daughter) we used this cottage as our base for my run of shows at the Edinburgh Festival. I would drive to Edinburgh each afternoon, do my show at 8 p.m. and then drive back to Bamburgh. Happy days and as I write this, I am reminded that Nikki brought baby Tom to see my show which was inappropriate because he couldn't understand and might have been distracting but also befitting since he had already inspired some of the best material in my act...

...my son doesn't sleep. He recharges. He's like a mobile phone. You plug him in for an hour, he's good for the whole day. During the day, I'll be knackered. I'll want to just sit down and read the newspaper and so I will appeal to my son. I'll say... 'Hey, listen... Nokia...'

Anyway, back to compatibility and why Mr and Mrs H always had a fighting chance.

Off the Northumberland coast is a series of islands including the famous Lindisfarne, also known as the Holy Island. Here a monastery was founded in 635 AD by Saint Aidan of Iona and where Christianity took root and began to flourish. Over the years, Nikki and I visited Lindisfarne frequently and became fond of the place.

Years later, strolling along the same beach with other friends, Nikki looked out to the ocean and pointed out the island.

"You see over there. That island in the distance... That's Lindisfarne."

Our friend's interest was piqued. He had probably heard of Lindisfarne but didn't know why. Something about a folk group? Or maybe something religious? Something spiritual anyway and he was pleased that Nikki was on hand to enlighten him.

"It's also known as The Holy Island..." Nikki continued and his intrigue grew. Holy how? Why? What happened there?

But Nikki had a pearl of much more gravity than anything a Saint had established centuries ago.

"...that's where I had my first Magnum."

That Nikki even remembered this and furthermore, that she thought it was worth sharing. Sure, we all like Magnums.

Who doesn't like a choc-ice? But is a first choc-ice really so momentous? Bigger even than the legacy of establishing Christianity in Europe.

If our friend was disappointed, he didn't show it. He burst out laughing and so did Nikki and I.

These days, people are mustard keen to appear learned and cerebral. But not me and certainly not Nikki.

We are aware of our shortcomings and are able to accommodate them easily enough. And this is partly why I reckon we've got miles left in the tank yet.

Take Five

For Free!

When I first heard of the FREE fringe I positively shuddered and assured myself that I would never do such a thing. Comedians performing for free with their audiences deciding how much money to donate (if anything?) as they exit the show and pass the performer holding an empty bucket.

In essence, indoor busking.

The indignity of such a thing. Never would I stoop so low. Not for me, thank you very much.

And yet my last two visits to the festival with my shows, *Eclipsed* and *The Glory Year*, were indeed free to attend. Each performance was full and my audience (in the main) understood the dynamics and their role and they duly coughed up. One giant transaction between the performer and a group of strangers, a business case study in itself and I reckon enough for PhDs in economics, sociology, philosophy and psychology.

It was thrilling for me and my boys to count the spoils after each show. It felt dangerous being laden with cash and furtively paying local restaurateurs with notes and heaps of coins, which presumably would not be fully accounted for by them either.

But I wonder how long the 'FREE' show can continue and not just because of the elimination of cash, which has been hastened by Covid and cedes even more control to our political masters.

More so because of psychology and the way that certain people behave when they aren't compelled to pay for something.

All free fringe performers must steel themselves for the unusual folk who will contribute nothing, whether they have enjoyed the show or not. These are not people who are necessarily strapped for cash. They simply don't contribute because paying nothing is an option. A peculiar type of person and I guess, the ultimate heckle.

Nothing queerer than folk as the adage has it and yet my indignation pales when I recently watched a performer with a much greater story than my own receiving an even starker slap in the face.

I was in Cape Town visiting Nikki and Paddy, where he happened to be filming a TV show called *Invasion*.

Film sets are spectacularly boring places, unless you have a role other than just being a parent. One morning I sloped off to visit Robben Island, the fortress outcrop where Nelson Mandela and other political prisoners of the apartheid era had been imprisoned.

Waiting for the ferry, I was keen to read the displays about the island's dark history and I felt chastened by my ignorance. Everyone is familiar with Nelson Mandela, but how about Robert Mangaliso Sobukwe?

Anyone?

No, me neither, which is something to ponder. He died at fifty-three, effectively incarcerated his entire adult life for his political beliefs. A remarkably brave and principled man.

For me and my fellow tourists, who hailed from across the globe, our trip to Robben Island was a history lesson and much else besides.

Our guide was Peter, a man I'd put in his late sixties. Peter had spent eighteen years as a prisoner on the island which is now his place of work. Funny how life pans out, eh?

In his own words:

"This prison is where I grew us."

And what a place it is.

Inmates were permitted two visits a year (thirty minutes maximum) with only English permitted so that the guards could monitor conversations. Because many inmates could only speak African languages, visits were reduced to staring and smiling only. And tears I imagine.

Peter was kindly and impassioned but his English was not so clear, nor very easy to hear with the popcorn munchers all around me.

Standing in the courtyard where Mandela had spent years crushing rocks, Peter pointed to the window of the future President's cell.

"...like all men here. In his cell, Mandela had just a mat. No bed. No pillow. A single blanket and a baguette..."

Making my way inside, I pondered the notion of a 'baguette' until I saw the bucket and I realised my error. It made me smile and provided some useful light relief.

President Mandela's cell and the whole prison is pristine now. Polished concrete floors, all swept and shipshape. But how must it have been when it was a working jail and crammed with prisoners? The pungent smell of sweat and excrement in the stifling heat would have been overwhelming. And only freezing seawater to slop out with and for the men to wash.

The whole experience was confusing. It prompted large philosophical questions which I was unable to address and only increased my sense of bewilderment. And yet things were about to become even more bleak.

At the end of the tour, Peter made a point of thanking us and instantly, it reminded me of the FREE fringe and how acts end their shows. In effect a plea to the audience to do the right thing.

In this case, even though we had paid for the tour, surely people would recognise Peter's circumstances and his gentle appeal and they might wish to thank him personally with something pressed into his hand.

Presumably, none of us have ever experienced similar hardships and it is unlikely that tourists to Cape Town are on a stringent budget. Europeans and Americans who are pinched tend not to vacation in South Africa.

So I was dumbfounded by how many people had only a "thank you" for Peter as they filed past him. I thought of Nelson Mandela and what he would have done. On his release from prison, Mandela surprised the world with his lack of recrimination and his pleas for healing. I think Mandela would have given Peter more than a nod and a thank you.

Putting on a show in Edinburgh is quite an undertaking. It requires a huge investment in time, money and emotions (darling). People enjoying the show for free (because they can) is irksome but nothing by comparison to what Peter had endured.

He had spent a third of his life in a living hell for people to merely funnel past him, probably thinking of their afternoon ahead and whether there is time for a cheeky chocolate bar without ruining their evening meal.

South African politics is a minefield, impossible to fathom and understand. But so was the mean-spiritedness I witnessed that day. This might be a good place to start in trying to understand how mankind is so capable but equally so wanting.

Take Six

The Perils of Life on the Road

Stand-up comedy is stressful enough without being late for a gig, as happened to me many moons ago in the proud city of Bristol. Pre-dating sat-navs and arriving late to the city hopelessly lost, I spied a pedestrian on the roadside and pulled over to plead for directions. Ordinarily I would have noticed that this chap was not a good prospect but as desperate as I was, I yelled through my window the address of where I needed to be. In my head, this was an emergency, because people were waiting for me to make them laugh.

The man stared at me and appeared to make a quick assessment.

"I'm going that way. Why don't I jump in and I can show you."

And to prove the extent of my hopelessness, I allowed this to happen. He got into my car and instantly I regretted it.

The first thing to hit me was the smell. A pungent odour I had never smelt before. It was acrid and overwhelming. I opened all the windows and hoped that he wouldn't reason why.

"Which way?" I pleaded.

But he had other things on his pickled mind, namely to explore the footwell of my car. This is when I noticed the gaping wound on the back of his head, his hair matted with blood old and new. A fierce yellow puss was oozing on to the blackened collar of his shirt. I worried that the puss might be his brains. Are brains yellow? And how might this affect his sense of direction? Because yes, dear reader, it was still all about me and my gig.

I continued to drive aimlessly hoping for a miracle, when suddenly he sat upright clutching a spent shotgun cartridge that he had found in my car. You can imagine my shock although there is a reasonable explanation for its presence which I won't go into here.

"Have you got a shotgun?"

His West Country accent seemed broader now and somehow more menacing because he was clearly under the influence of something other than oxygen and my panic ramped up further.

"No." I replied, scared shitless and furious with myself.

"Do you want one?" he asked.

No. I didn't want a gun. I just wanted to get to my gig and tell my jokes. Hopefully people would laugh and then I could drive home to my wife and kids. I'm a dad. I have kids and they need me…

He began rummaging about in his holdall, presumably for a gun and now my gig is long-forgotten, replaced by much more pressing matters, like staying alive. My options were dwindling and none of them were good.

Comedians run the risk of getting no laughs on stage, something we refer to as dying. An awful prospect for any stand-up but infinitely preferable to, you know, actually dying. I now seriously contemplated just stopping my car and running. I was confident I could outrun him and if he did shoot, I was pretty sure he would miss.

He continued to wrestle with his holdall and I could barely look. One eye on the road and the other on a potential murder weapon. Surely, his bag was too small to house a normal shotgun but what about a sawn-off? By now, I decided that I would cede to whatever demands he made. He can have all my money. My mobile phone and even my car. But I would draw the line at any sexual favours. A bridge too far.

Finally, after an almighty tussle, he managed to release the object from his bag, which he duly pointed at me but thankfully it wasn't a gun…

But a leg of lamb.

I kid you not.

Here I was, lost in Bristol. Late for my gig. With a homeless man in my car pointing a leg of lamb at me.

This was when I noticed his hands. They were badly swollen and an array of colours. Bright pink to black and every hue in-between. His fingers were fat, like bananas. His knuckles were mostly ripped open. What nails he had left were black. Old injuries compounded by new, the guy was quite literally rotting and now I understood the smell.

"Do you wanna buy a leg of lamb?"

This ranks as the most bizarre question I have ever been asked in my life.

He continued with his sales pitch.

"I've just burgled it from Sainsbury's…"

I didn't think to correct his English. Burgle might be a verb in the sense that a house can be burgled. But a leg of lamb cannot be burgled. A leg of lamb can be stolen or purloined but not burgled.

"Twenty quid in the shop. But you can have it for a tenner…"

Clearly, this was a good deal. Half price, plus I get to survive. I daresay I could have hung on for an even better deal.

£7.50?

But of course, my survival instincts kicked in.

Back in the day, when heading to gigs, I would leave my wallet at home and just take a twenty pound note to cover any petrol, food or any other emergencies and this most certainly was an emergency.

Deftly, I produced the note. His blood shot, yellowing eyes focussed slowly and then widened.

"Stop the car."

I duly obliged. He grabbed the money and practically fell out of my car, possibly adding further injuries to his already stricken body. And then he was gone. On his toes, no doubt to buy something to take him out of his consciousness and who can blame the poor wretch.

The only thing that remained of him was the terrible stench (the smell of imminent death, I fear) and true to his word, the leg of lamb.

I could have cried with happiness. I was tempted to call Nikki to tell her that I was alive.

But then I remembered the gig and reality reasserted itself. Never mind being alive and married with three kids. There were people waiting for me and I needed to be funny...

*

I made the gig.

I know this, because I have never missed a gig in my entire career. An absence of sick pay might have some bearing here. But I cannot recall how I fared. And I have no recollection either what became of the leg of lamb but I suspect we didn't eat it.

Take Seven

Gear Grinding

There are lots of markers in life. Little things that punctuate our time on Earth and flag the passing of the years. Some are obvious, like a creaking hip or a receding hairline. Others are more creeping and subtle, like becoming forgetful and irate. And some are completely oblique and catch us unawares, like my increasing disappointment at the efficiency of the pepper grinder.

I am unclear if this is because I have developed such a voracious appetite for pepper that my grinder can't keep pace with it, or that I just happen to have a particularly inefficient device.

I grew up with salt and pepper cellars which contained pre-ground spices and were highly efficient at delivering seasoning. These cellars did not need to be reinvented and yet somehow they have made way for the much more troublesome and inefficient grinders.

My current pepper grinder is a huge disappointment to me and yes, I am aware that this is a First World problem and indicates a cossetted life. Maybe so, but everything is relative and I feel a pressing need to vent on just how irksome my pepper mill is.

Where to begin…

Well, it's brand new to start with and it happened to be the most expensive model available in my local branch of John Lewis. Purchased during lockdown because its predecessor was useless and my boiled eggs were remaining too white. But my new peppermill is little better. And doubly frustrating since it happens to have a clear body, which means I can see the peppercorns that are not being ground, as though the bloody thing is tormenting me.

Of course, I could return the wretched thing to John Lewis but this goes against my nature. Our high street is under enough pressure from online retailers; the last thing they need is its loyal customers turning on them.

A moral stand then?

Yes, to a point, but also because I have not kept the receipt, why would I? What sort of person keeps the proof of purchase for a pepper grinder?

I might be able to retrieve such a thing for a larger ticket item. Something like a television, though note here the use of the word 'might'. But never for a pepper mill. Just how organised is the person who not only retains such a receipt, but also has a place for it should it ever be needed?

And on this quandary, I discovered something remarkable about my new pepper mill and human quirkiness.

One morning, eating my disappointing eggs, I was studying my mill in the hope of understanding why it can grind my gears but not my peppercorns.

On the underside of the pepper mill I found a translucent sticker with two extraordinary words...

"Lifetime Guarantee"

Wow.

Guaranteed for life!

Talk about overconfidence. Like rubbing seasoning into my wound. And this got me thinking about the sort of person who might act on such a long and generous guarantee...

The sort of person who keeps the receipt to begin with and has a place for it, remembers where this place is and crucially, is happy to call it in, even if they made the purchase in 1956. A stance which might be technically correct and within the law but will never be a reasonable thing to do. It is not something I would ever do because I have a sense of dignity and an instinct for doing the right thing.

My dad used to tell me that from the moment we are born, we learn right from wrong and that by doing so, we become human beings.

It is a basic human requirement to know what is right and what is wrong and if bland eggs are the price of this, then so be it.

Take Eight

Pain Killer

Pain is unpleasant but necessary. A necessary evil. An essential part of our body's defence system. Pain keeps us safe. A child will only touch a hot stove once. And when we do get burnt, the accompanying pain demands that we attend to the injury.

A foot injury is accompanied by sufficient pain that we avoid load bearing until such time that the foot is repaired and can be used again.

But although pain has this important function, we can choose to ignore it. We can choose to endure pain for what we perceive to be a greater good and most often, this is for vanity and a desire to look good.

An extreme example of this is elective surgery. Having things inserted into the body (cheek bones, chin dimples, all manner of gels and silicones) or having things removed (fat, a rib, excess skin…) and any number of other procedures.

These measures are drastic and, I venture, do not provide the individuals with the lives they crave.

But there is a much more common example of pain endurance in the pursuit of being more desirable.

The high heeled shoe.

I have no experience of painful shoes but I am aware of what instruments of torture they are to achieve a lengthened leg and a hallowed slimmer calf.

Hmm...

Childbirth is accepted to be the greatest pain a human being ever encounters and for this, all men should pay all women infinite respect. Back in the day, I used to do a stand-up routine arguing that the most painful thing a human endures is when we tread barefoot onto an unturned plug. After welcoming my first-born into the world, I continued with the routine but I added...

'...in fact, the greatest pain a human can endure - is a woman giving birth, whilst standing on a plug.'

I do not have a high pain threshold. I can be laid low by a single mouth ulcer, and I have a peculiar need to show people (Nikki) the offending white blemish, presumably to elicit sympathy.

So I would never wear shoes that hurt me, no matter how much taller (and more attractive?) they made me.

But women must be braver (or vainer?) than men and that explains why they need two sets of shoes for a night out. Comfy, 'on-their-way-to-the-event' shoes and 'instruments-of-torture-minx' shoes to change into.

At black tie dinners where I am speaking, the holding room where I sit and prepare can be a place to behold when it doubles as the organisers on-site office. Young women, having worked the ballroom selling raffle tickets suddenly crash through the doors and immediately kick off their shoes and clutch their aching feet. The doorway becomes like the threshold to a bouncy castle with shoes discarded everywhere.

And I wish I had known this in my youth when the phrase that troubled me was…

Tall, dark and handsome.

I had only one of these attributes and I knew that it was the bronze medal of the three.

But in my formative years, words even more frightening than these were simply…

"Would you like to dance?"

The question that terrorised boys like me at the school disco.

If only I had known then what I know now…

That girls at school discos are highly likely to be in considerable pain. If I had known this, then I could have avoided this ghastly question altogether and even turned it to my advantage.

I could have sidled up to an unsuspecting girl on the dance floor and popped a question she wasn't expecting but might really appreciate…

"…would you like to sit down?"

Take Nine

Tea is Home

Over the years I have accumulated hours of stand-up routines which when recited correctly and with the right intonation, make people laugh out loud.

Comedy 'gold' as I call them but this is subjective of course. My Edinburgh show in 2018, *Eclipsed* was awarded an insulting two stars by *The Daily Telegraph* which I processed easily enough since the critic was dressed like Oscar Wilde (complete with scarf) so his opinion is suitably diminished.

Never afraid to take on contentious subjects, one of my favourite routines (gold?) focussed on the English obsession with tea which began something like this…

…my name is Dominic but people call me Dom. I am English. Born in England. Lived in England all my life. This makes me English and what this means… is that in any given day, I drink more tea than I actually enjoy…

Boom!

Okay, it might be less funny in print. But it worked on stage and is on YouTube if you need proof.

Like many Englishmen, I love tea.

It is my go-to drink… or at least it is when I can make it myself because I am very particular about my tea. Everything is important, even the cup which must be thin and preferably China.

There are few things worse than tea served in an earthenware mug.

"…you take a load off and I'll make us both a nice cup of lukewarm tea…"

Such offending mugs are frequently sold in craft shops and are usually the size of a small bucket which is too much tea for anyone, even the English.

And then to the tea making process itself, which is crucial.

Teapot users, I salute you and I do not criticise your old fashioned ways. I have only fond memories of my school holidays in Ireland and the Isle of Man which featured ranges and huge pots of tea but that was a process of its time and I have moved on.

The same affection goes to the loose tea aficionados amongst you, complete with your strainers. Organised types I imagine, the sort of person who might keep the receipt for a pepper grinder.

I am however, a tea bag man and 'builders' brew is my preference, which denotes the colour (not the sweetness) and is achieved as follows…

Bag in cup. Add boiling water. Leave to brew while a spoon

is retrieved to stir and squeeze bag against the cup. Discard bag straight into bin or preferably a food waste caddy (middle class) and then add milk, semi-skimmed and not too much. Just enough to turn the tea a malty brown.

I even stipulate a brand of tea (Yorkshire) and all of these strict stipulations mean I rarely agree to tea being made for me. It is just too risky.

These issues are even more pronounced when I am abroad. Even if I have brought tea bags with me, I just can't make the tea I enjoy at home. Perhaps it's the water or maybe the milk, I don't know. Or its physics and water doesn't boil the same as it does back home?

Or it might be none of these.

It could be psychosomatic. It could be that the tea is in fact the same. It's just that the place is different and the issue is my hankering for home.

An Englishman's home is his castle as the expression goes.

But a castle, no matter how grand, only becomes a home with a hot cup of tea.

*

In line with *Take One*, keener readers might have noticed my mention of a brand in this *Take*. A gratuitous inclusion and a flagrant attempt to receive free stuff, in this instance, tea bags.

On this charge, I plead guilty.

Take Ten

Men and Motors

It would not have happened had I been better organised, or if I had read the emails, or my contract or paid attention to the briefing call that came with the gig I had been booked for. But I know best and as it transpired, I knew nothing at all as I drove out of London heading North. Armed only with my talent, a suit to change into and a vague destination of Northampton-ish.

A hotel most likely but I would know soon enough when my sat-nav announces…

You have arrived at your destination.

And waiting for me will be a bunch of people who I am charged with making laugh without tickling anyone. An unusual job, but there we are.

Proceeding up the motorway, (freeway, highway - international readership!), on my radio was an excited discussion about the British Grand Prix taking place over the weekend at the famous Silverstone race track. This was of no interest to me and I zoned out, until I saw a road sign for Silverstone and something shifted in my dusty brain.

Two words occurred to me: 'Hewlett' and 'Packard', the American tech giant, long since known as HP because presumably life is just too short.

You know the company. The printer people. Like tattooists, they make their money out of ink and I had a sneaky feeling that HP were the company expecting a funny man. And since Hewlett Packard were a prominent sponsor of the Williams F1 team, everything began to click into place.

I'm doing a gig at the British Grand Prix and it humoured me that I would arrive in my turquoise Fiat Multipla (Google it), a car not known for its aerodynamics or speed.

Eventually I left the motorway as instructed. I was closing in on my venue and I continued to chuckle. I have good comedy routines on the Grand Prix and on printers and I sensed that the gig would be a triumph, darling.

The venue was indeed a hotel. A purpose-built monstrosity close to the circuit and large enough to accommodate all the drivers, their teams, sponsors and journalists under one hideous roof.

I arrived in plenty of time for the gig but not early enough to avoid being completely humiliated.

I knew things were awry as soon as I drew up to the hotel gates. This being a gaudy hotel of Disneyesque proportions, there was a very long drive from the road. Outside the gates was a line (queue) of cars and being polite and English, I duly joined the back.

Not unusual that the hotel was full and busy on race weekend.

But what was unusual, however, were the cars ahead of me: Lamborghinis, Ferraris, Aston Martins… maybe ten cars including mine and mine was the only one with a velour interior and three seats in the front.

I nudged forward as another car rounded the entrance and was greeted by a large cheer.

How strange.

I started to wonder and I started to fret.

I called the client to let them know I'd arrived but that I was stuck in this illustrious line of cars. The client explained something about an exhibition of the world's most famous road cars, would make some calls and come back to me…

At this juncture, what I hadn't realised was that both sides of the one mile driveway to the Happy Eater hotel were lined with race fans. Maybe a thousand people, mainly men with a penchant for cars that roar and turn heads. Just like the vehicles ahead of me. Cars that have won Le Mans and other famous races. Everything was carefully orchestrated with cars in specific order according to the accompanying brochure for the enthusiasts to reference. In addition, there was an announcer welcoming each growler on to the tarmac. You know the kind of thing…

"…next up is a 1962 Lamborghini big-swinging-dick, V12, 8 cylinder, 6000 horse power…"

Upon which the petrolheads (men) screamed their approval.

My phone rings. It's the client and it's not great news.

"They're going to stop the rally, so you can drive in…"

No other entrance available, I take it? You know, a less humiliating one.

A man in a hi-vis jacket got off his radio and smiled broadly as he beckoned me forward, one hand raised to keep the next souped-up racehorse at bay…

Obviously, I wasn't in the brochure and I didn't get an announcement either.

"Ladies and Gentlemen, next up is a 1.8 litre diesel Fiat Multipla. Unusual in aqua marine. Ideal for the virile man with more kids than he can realistically afford…"

As I rounded the corner, I saw the crowd for the first time and my spirits plummeted.

Not that I wasn't welcome. Au contraire. Judging by the grins and hoots of derision, my people carrier was an instant hit. But what I couldn't have known was that the cars before me had circumvented the speed restricting humps with doughnuts and wheel spins. So, I must have looked even more pathetic, obediently negotiating each speed hump in second gear. An already conspicuous car made even more apparent.

I also didn't realise that within the crowds were the very people who I would face at my gig. So, you could reason that I had started work early because I got plenty of laughs, albeit at me and not with me.

But in my game, a laugh is a laugh and I duly fired off my invoice for merriment rendered whether it was intended or not.

What sane person would ever think being funny is a good way to make a living?

*

In line with Take One and Take Nine, some readers may have noted my inclusion of a number of brand names in this Take, namely, Lamborghini, Ferrari and Aston Martin and yes, this is another flagrant and cynical…

Take Eleven

Craft Work

In *Take Nine – Tea is Home* - I did not mean to give the impression that I am against craft shops and their wares. Quite the opposite is true. I love craft and craftmanship. I admire anyone who can make things and enjoy supporting their work, particularly so when I am abroad.

Tourists are easy prey of course and are vulnerable to making unwise purchases. A little something to remember a place by. An item to lock in a memory and perhaps act as a conversation starter back home.

I am particularly partial to things that have been made by local artisans, although I am wary since I never seem to see anything being sculpted, woven, carved or painted and I worry that a factory in China, possibly staffed by slaves might well be the source.

But leaving such cynicism aside and hoping that there are indigenous artists fashioning beautiful wares from local materials, then I am all-in and fully supportive.

I admire their skill and imagination, not to mention their hard work carving something so intricate from something as unyielding as stone. The ingenuity also. A lump of wood that can be burnt as a heat source or be carved into an animal and sold for a comparative fortune.

It is easy to admire such endeavour and I became especially vulnerable on my three trips to Africa, visiting Namibia, Kenya and most recently, South Africa.

To remember my trips but also to support people much less fortunate than myself and why I don't like to barter. Who wants to haggle over a few pounds with a man who lives in a hut and sleeps on the ground? Perhaps the sort of person who watches a FREE show in Edinburgh and takes it literally!

I am easily drawn to an animal carving. My bathroom wall is festooned with elephants, rhinos, buffalo… each a reminder of a place and a time and hopefully carved by hand and not by a lathe in China.

Nairobi's Kibera is the largest slum dwelling in sub-Saharan Africa. Life expectancy is half what we can expect in London and this is partly because no bank will finance the exploitation of their natural mineral reserves as a source of fuel. The people are confined to burning wood and dried dung in their huts, the fumes from which poison their lungs not to mention the frequent accidents, burns and fires.

I am reminded of this unpleasant fact every time I have a bath and this is a problem because baths are supposed to be relaxing. The people of Kibera do not have toilets, let alone baths. And if they did have baths, they could not fill them with hot water because unlike me, they are not allowed to burn gas.

Life is definitely not fair.

A bath is where I do a lot of my thinking. Stories I am writing or routines I can tell on-stage. When I am home alone, I am very happy lying in the bath, chatting away to myself or just pondering. Just me and my array of carved animals.

On the wall opposite me (above the taps) are three elephants walking in line. Above them is a muscular rhino and next is some sort of bovine creature. An oryx maybe?

And looking at them now, a thought occurs to me that makes me smile. What any prospective purchaser of an animal carving must always keep in mind is this…

…that no matter how carefully the carving is wrapped and transported home, it is advisable to imagine what the animal will look like with a tusk missing, a broken trunk or even a missing tail.

Take Twelve

Alpine Vice

This *Take* can serve as an admission, an apology or even a lesson depending on your personal moral compass.

Nikki and I, along with our boys, decamped one year for a week's holiday to a French ski chalet. The exception was Sam because he was working in the same ski resort as a chalet host. A full-on job waiting hand and foot on his guests: cleaning the chalet, preparing breakfast and an evening meal plus afternoon cakes and tea. Such holidays are not cheap but little of the money shelled out by the clients trickles down as far as the chalet hosts.

Sam was nineteen and away from home for the first time. A steep learning curve and life lesson with the princely salary of £75 per week to go with his room and board.

When we arrived it was exciting to see him although he looked weary and a little thin.

'Dad, we start at 6am on cooked breakfasts. We clean all day and then don't finish the evening meal until gone 9 p.m., so there's not much time to eat.'

Mmm…

That said, there's nothing wrong with putting in a shift. Some of the company's other chalet hosts had thrown in the towel already and I was pleased that Sam and his co-host, Ben, were making a good fist of it. Guest feedback in their exit questionnaires was fulsome with praise.

"Excellent food. Chalet spotless. Excellent hosts."

'And what about tips?' I asked expectantly, keen to find other upsides to accompany the aforementioned life lesson. Sam looked at me blankly.

Back at team Holland's chalet, our hosts were a young couple. She was Dutch, he was Irish. Old for hosts – early 30's – but chasing tourists the year-round, so they could see the world and save some money. They were excellent. In from our days skiing, he would have a fire waiting for us and she was a superb cook. I noted on the wall a display of thank you letters written by their previous guests.

And this gave me a fiendish idea.

From a local shop, I bought some writing paper and an array of different coloured pens and I charged each Holland to write letters of gratitude from nom de plume for Sam and Ben to hang in their chalet. And boy, did they rise to this challenge.

"Dear Sam and Ben,

Wow… What a week… Thank you soooo much…"

And following such gush, the crucial line included in each fake letter…

"Enclosed is a little thank you from us all."

Ever thorough, I even bought Blu Tack for affixing purposes. Sam and Ben duly plastered their dining room wall and what do you think happened?

Firstly, guests began to write and leave genuine letters of gratitude and included the all-important monetary thank you, which made all the difference to the experience of two young lads working their tails off.

I am no lawyer but this ploy was definitely misleading. It might even be a crime. Fraud, deception, even theft?

And if so, then I am guilty as charged. I offer an apology to any guests at Sam's chalet who might have felt coerced (I prefer coaxed) into coughing up. Although, that they needed such encouragement is something to reflect on.

And finally, to the lesson of this short *Take*, which is simply this…

Of course it is not good to lie. It is always better to be honest. This is a value drummed into us as children. A worthy principle we should try to adhere to throughout our lives.

But not always.

Because sometimes we are required to lie…

At a dinner party when a meal has been cooked for us.

When someone has a daring new hair style.

And when two young kids are getting stiffed by rich (comparatively) holiday makers on a skiing jaunt.

At the end of their season, Sam and Ben won the highest scores of any of the chalet hosts in their company. All down to their hard work, albeit aided and abetted by highly devious and mischievous but deeply caring parents.

Sam's delight in phoning us with his news of their victory remains one of my proudest dad moments.

And to this end and whilst we are on the subject of sinning…

Nikki enjoyed this *Take* although she took issue with it, though not for the reason you might imagine. Namely that we are exposing our own deception, not to mention the good name of our son.

No, no. She had no problem with that. Or rather she did, but not the exposure per se.

"That was my idea." she claimed proudly.

It's one thing being deceptive and cunning, but demanding credit for such a thing and in such a public forum like a book and a podcast is a whole new level of vice - a level I feel a need to distance myself from.

Take Thirteen

A Numerical Humbling

In this *Take* I present an abiding memory and one which says so much about me.

I am eleven years old, in my first year of senior school, have been assigned to a class of no-hopers, so there is much riding on my first examination. A chance then to exonerate myself, but unfortunately, it happens to be in mathematics.

Our teacher is Mr Chmai.

A great big bear of a man with a granite face, he made little secret that his life and career had not panned out as he had hoped. With his thick Polish accent and always wearing a gown, he was frankly terrifying but I loved him. I admired him too, not least because he had survived a Nazi concentration camp and had the tattoo on his wrist for all to see.

The exam was general arithmetic with sixty-five marks on offer. This number is important so do keep it in mind.

The examination was a cinch. So easy, I completed it with time to spare as less able boys around me continued to struggle. I assured my mum that I had aced the exam and immediately she fretted.

"Oh, no, Dom thinks he's done well. Dom never does well when he thinks he's done well!"

On results day, Mr Chmai appeared in a particularly dark mood as he flung our papers down, shaking his head in pain and torment. He might have survived the Nazis but it appeared that class 1M of Cardinal Vaughan school might be the death of him.

But this didn't trouble me at all. If anything, I was delighted that my classmates had fared so badly because it would make my stellar performance even more impressive.

"….I have your examination results…"

Mr Chmai said with derision. He might as well have added "… *you bunch of losers"*

"I will read out the results in descending order. As you hear your name, come and retrieve your paper…"

At this, I was poised and ready like a sprinter in the blocks.

"In first place, with fifty-six points…"

This immediately dented my sail because whilst I was happy to finish first, fifty-six points was a much lower score than I had expected. How had I forfeited so many marks? Only fifty-six out of sixty-five, that's er… hang on…

"Benedict Eadle"

As my classmate Benedict recovered his paper and presumably

the teacher's congratulations, I was reeling in shock. I hadn't come first and by now I had established that the winning paper had missed out on nine marks.

"In second place with fifty-four... Timothy Byrne..."

My jaw slackened. Not even second place?

And my bewilderment grew as we proceeded down in scores. Into the forties and still I remained seated and wondering if a mistake hadn't been made.

Into the thirties and now I was shifting awkwardly.

Frank Murphy came in with a score of thirty-three – a pivotal number in this particular equation – because if you recall, the total marks on offer was sixty-five. If you can't see the significance of thirty-three then I am afraid that you are even more stupid than me and you are unlikely to ever set the world alight.

Thirty-three, thirty-two, thirty-one....

Down he continued and by now my confusion had been replaced by fear – praying that my name might be next.

Into the twenties and still no Dominic Holland.

The twenties quickly ran out quickly and we were into the teens. I was ashen. Everything was a blur. Rational thought had gone as I watched boys retrieving their papers with scores of sixteen and fifteen and I felt envious of them.

And then we got to ten, another pivotal number; my last chance of a two-digit score. The lucky bastard with this accolade was John O'Connor, a nice kid with red hair but in a school of Irish Catholics, this was not noteworthy.

And then, something truly beautiful happened.

Ian Porter was sitting to my left. Ian was a scamp of a lad from the East End of London. He was cackling wildly at our friend O'Connor.

"…here, Dom, look at O'Connor. Jeez man, ten! How thick is he?"

The question was a welcome distraction but it confused me because I was not aware that Ian had retrieved his paper yet. I asked him what he had scored.

"Dunno. I aint been called out yet."

As funny as this was, I couldn't laugh at the time. I had other things on my mind.

And finally it came.

"DOMINIC HOLLAND"

NINE.

On my way to Mr. Chmai's desk, already at play is a rare 'gift' that I possess.

Delusional Optimism.

Finally on my feet, I assured myself that I had not finished last. God Bless, Ian Porter. And that whilst nine is not a great score, it is better than eight, and…

But unfortunately, my dad was more of a realist and wept at his careless son's errors.

And yet this harrowing tale would provide an extraordinary upside in years to come…

Some three decades on, my school contacted me regarding their centenary celebrations and requested that I might speak at the event. Suitably flattered and eager to please, I quickly agreed. I heard the word 'Hall' and had visions of the school hall where I gave my first comic speech when I was seventeen. I liked the idea of revisiting my debut venue, this time with a little more stage time to lean on.

The 'hall' however, happened to be The Royal Albert Hall, the world-famous concert venue in London.

Back stage was a reckoning for me as the only 'old boy' on the bill. No doubt, others had been approached; boys who had become more illustrious adults than me but who were sensible enough to decline the offer to speak and instead had taken their seats in the comfortable auditorium while stupid Holland stood backstage shitting himself.

The place was fit to burst with five thousand people including the entire current school and staff sitting in the stalls. Ex staff and old boys, parents (including my own) and many others besides and me having to speak for ten minutes or so.

What better story to tell than my ignominious first maths exam? What I hadn't accounted for was that a great number of the audience had also been taught by Mr Chmai who had long since died. When I first mentioned his name on stage, something really quite wonderful happened. A wave of affection caught hold of the hallowed hall and while it delighted me, I admonished myself for not anticipating it. Everyone loved Mr Chmai and everyone loved hearing my tale.

The misery of my paltry score came to my rescue over three

decades later in an opportunity to make my entire school laugh and in the august Royal Albert Hall. Quite a beautiful thing really and proof that there are always upsides to everything no matter how bleak things appear at the time. We just have to look for them and sometimes be very, very patient.

Take Fourteen

Old Memory Lane

You may have heard about the recent medical breakthrough in battling Alzheimer's although whether this news registered with you is probably a factor of your age.

I could joke that I have forgotten already what this actual breakthrough is, but memory loss is no laughing matter and particularly for people like me who recognise the signs of their hard drive failings. My younger sister regularly tells me about things from our childhood, things I said and did but I can't recall, and I have to take her word for it.

All boys and most men will spend some time developing their muscles, with most attention given to the biceps, but since memory is also a muscle and can be trained, it is a muscle we are foolish to disregard.

Which is why I am pleased that Nikki has announced she is relearning French. A positive thing to do on so many levels. Having English as our mother tongue is a great advantage of course, but a disadvantage also because it allows us to become lazy. French is the most melodic and beautiful language and it is a good thing also to prove that old dogs can in fact learn new tricks. Learning a new language is a big hurdle to straddle, but it is good for the brain and for the soul.

Indeed, I am tempted to join her, if only to exercise my memory muscle because there is little chance of me mastering French given my inglorious attempts as a schoolboy.

On holiday in France when our boys were very young, we rented a quaint farmhouse in the middle of nowhere. While the owner showed us around and pointed out the do's and don'ts, I suggested to Nikki that I might take a drive to the nearest town to get a food shop; maybe some choc-ices for the kids and some brownie points for the dad.

What could possibly go wrong?

Well, I could complete the food shop and then get completely and hopelessly lost…

Driving out of the town repeatedly, taking different roads each time and hoping to see something familiar, but making no headway, I decided I should stop and ask for directions.

My six years of French lessons were about to come in very handy indeed.

I approached a couple of middle aged ladies nattering over the fence of their front gardens. As I approached I realised that I had very little to go on. Not an address, the owners name and I didn't have much French either.

I opened strongly with...

"Bonjour."

Both women looked at me curiously.

I followed up hello, with...

"Excusez-moi, je suis Anglaise..."

"Excuse me, I am English" – to which I added my best smile in the hope of buying myself a little more time.

All I had to share was that I was looking for a house which is owned by a small French man. What I needed to explain was that I was renting a farmhouse from this small French man in the hope that this would be enough. That the ladies would recognise the house and my plight and kindly direct me home.

You can see now that this was always a long-shot and even more unlikely given my limited French.

"J'habite en maison..."

"I live in a house" – which is the best I could do because I didn't know the verb to rent. I also did not know the word for owner but I thought the word 'proprietor' made a lot of sense because it sounds French.

"ou (where), le prop-rie-a-tuer est une petite..."

I should have got 'homme' for man – but in my panic I plumped for 'garcon' which is boy.

Without the small proprietors name, I now needed to describe him and well enough so that the French ladies might recognise him. I had already informed them that he was small and I recalled that he had a comparatively large nose.

"ou (where), le prop-rie-a-tor (the owner) est (is) une petite garcon (a small boy) avec un grande (with a big…)

Unfortunately, I could not recall nose in French, so I went default, saying nose with a heavy French accent whilst pointing to my nose (which is small) and gesturing a large hooter with my hand.

So to recap then…

I am lost in France. I approach two middle-aged French women and ask for directions with the following…

"Hello, excuse me. I am English. I live in a house where the owner is a small boy with a big nose."

Needless to say, they stared at me blankly, probably wondering whether they should call the police or an ambulance.

I did eventually find the house and my family. Nikki was pleased to see me but my boys less so because the choc-ices were no longer.

An epic dad fail in their eyes – and perhaps a foretaste of things to come.

I remember this incident vividly which I suppose offers me some solace about my ailing memory. But a further concern is that I seem to be capable of only recalling tales of my ignominy and woe. There must have been occasional victories in my past, little life-wins for me to draw on. Yes, of course, but these don't play well in a book like this. Laughs are had by going under the bus, not in it.

That said, I do intend to address my ailing memory muscle and make a plan for its work out. Crosswords, puzzles, maybe even learning something new. But I must not expect too much of myself. I am no spring chicken. Old dog and new tricks. And things do go wrong for us all, of course they so. Such is life.

Or perhaps a more appropriate way to say this and conclude this *Take* might be,

C'est la vie.

Take Fifteen

First Impressions Count…

I did my first ever one man show in 1993 and it featured a routine about the contrasts between the bladder and the bowel. How the bladder is a lot more uptight and demanding. How the bowel can be put off from being emptied if the moment does not suit us but the bladder is much less amenable.

If anything, the bladder is more anal which I proved in my thesis by posing this question, "how many of us are regularly woken up at night, dying for a poo?"

I described the bowel as an altogether more relaxed and chilled organ, with its kindly alerts that things are getting crowded down below. Suggestions rather than orders that a visit to the smallest room in the house is required. Notice being given rather than a demand that a visit to the loo is pending.

However, the bowel is relaxed only to a point. It will only take so many deferrals, before its patience snaps and it announces an immediate evacuation.

My exact words in the routine were something like…

"…but the bowel can only take so much shit."

And with this in mind, I recount an episode in my pre-comedy working life as a hapless salesman.

The first appointment for any sales rep is crucial. First impressions count and I was keen to do well. Dressed smartly in my only suit, I drove from my flat-share in Ealing to Edmonton for my first visit to a company called Bush Boake Allen. An unusual name and one I am unlikely to ever forget.

My route was a notoriously congested road and the sense of unknowing added to my anxiety and might have heightened the perfect storm I was driving into. I don't like tardiness. Quickly I become stressed when I am late. Especially so for an important meeting and unbeknownst to me, pressures are building within. This was before sat-navs and the strains of relying on a paper map added to the maelstrom ahead.

The first rumblings within did not worry me. This was the gentle nudge phase - a suggestion from bowel HQ and I returned a memo of my own…

Driving to an important meeting. Not convenient. Stand down.

But within twenty minutes or so, the rumblings had become more pressing, literally. My eyes were wide now and probably remained so. My buttocks clenched as I picked up speed scanning the road ahead for any opportunities for an evacuation. A McDonald's would have appeared like a desert oasis.

I entered the car park of Bush Boake Allen like the getaway car in an episode of Starsky and Hutch. I threw my car into a reserved space for a BBA executive. The CEO perhaps, I didn't care. With no time to pull on my jacket or retrieve my suitcase I tore into the building.

Reception was busy, of course. Other reps were already waiting, flicking through magazines, sipping coffee and none of them looked like their backsides were about to explode.

I was sweating profusely. Even Prince Andrew would have been sweating in such circumstances (he can't sweat, by the way).

Protocol is that a sales rep approaches the desk and waits for eye contact before announcing oneself, one's company and the person with whom one has an appointment.

"WHERE'S THE TOILET?" I blurted desperately.

Adding to my torture, the nearest toilet was through a set of double doors and at the end of a large open plan office, busy with people working when suddenly these doors burst open, whereupon a small man with a crazed expression appeared, sprinted through the office, kicked the toilet door down and disappeared inside.

Had the stalls been occupied I would have had no choice but to use a sink.

And as I sat there, any momentary thoughts of relief were repelled by having to re-emerge and quite possibly walk past the individual I was due to meet. If so, they might appreciate a fist bump rather than a handshake.

That walk through the office with all eyes on me was awkward. I don't recall how my meeting went but no doubt, I left my mark.

Driving home, I imagined how the employees must have laughed and enjoyed my visit. Unintentionally making people laugh probably made me wonder if I ought to try my hand at being funny for cash.

Whatever this *Take* says about us, breaking wind is always funny and so too are bowel malfunctions, even if they are vulgar and a lazy device for humour. And so, it does not augur well, when such things are used as a plot device by a novelist. I feel a need to warn those of you who are enjoying *Takes Vol. 2* so much that you're considering one of my unputdownable and hilarious novels...

Open Links and *I, Gabriel* both hinge on a bowel evacuation, so perhaps more discerning readers might wish to avoid them. However, all of my other novels are poo free and well worth a punt.

Take Sixteen

Shumbly Blumbly

With a score of 96% in my chemistry mock O-level, our teacher marked me out for a special mention.

First in class. The top man. A career in medicine perhaps?

It didn't occur to our teacher that providing us with the examination paper beforehand had anything to do with my stellar performance. Even more remarkably, it didn't occur to me either as I basked in the fleeting glory.

Idly I began to dream of what I might do with my life. Already, I had an idea that 'funny' was the only thing I felt proficient at but now with 96% in chemistry, perhaps I was underselling myself? At the time, I had a vague notion that chemistry is the essence of all life on Earth, and I had a gift for it, who knew?

Heady stuff, indeed.

A few weeks later I sat the actual exam and I failed. We all did. The entire class. Two years of teaching by a professional chemistry teacher and not one of us managed to get over the line. My grade

'E' brought things sharply into focus. My hopes of becoming a surgeon dashed and my 'funniness' became more pressing.

Not that I didn't enjoy the sciences. Indeed, one of my fondest childhood memories occurred in a chemistry class.

A different teacher this time who was writing on the blackboard. We were instructed to copy the words and formulae down verbatim and somehow magically understand it. By osmosis, perhaps, or is that biology?

I was sitting at the back of the class next to a kid called Sean Connor. Sean was a tough Irish kid who would shortly be expelled and I haven't seen him since.

Rather than copy from the board, Sean found it easier to copy down my work and this gave me an idea. I wondered if he might copy anything that I write? And never mind if this might impinge on my education and my prospects of a career in medicine.

I began cautiously by changing odd words but staying within the world of science. So, potassium became ammonia. Copper sulphate became copper manganese.

Sean duly copied and emboldened, I quickly progressed…

I have always had a thing for words and particularly so for making up my own. I am partial to rhyming, which drove my kids mad as they grew up with their quirky dad.

Shumbly blumbly was my favourite expression. A made-up word I still use almost every day which I feel a need to explain.

Whatever document I am working on – a novel, blog, essay… I use the word *shumbly* to mark where I am in the text. Since there will only be one *shumbly*, it can be easily located and I can resume writing.

With Sean scribbling away, suddenly he frowned.

"What does that say?"

"*Shumbly Blumbly*." I managed without giving myself away.

Sean's brow furrowed even more.

"What does that mean?"

"I don't know, Sean. It's chemistry…"

This was enough for my friend and he dutifully copied it down.

What happened next is a thing of school days wonder.

There must have been a commotion – probably my laughter – for the teacher to be sufficiently riled to single out Sean.

"Connor. What is going on, back there?"

"Nothing, Miss."

"Then read out to the class the last few sentences you've written."

I listened with glee as Sean read out my chemistry mash-up, mixing elements and compounds with atoms and acids…

And when he finally got to '*Shumbly Blumbly*', we were both turfed out to see the headmaster.

What I had done was sacrifice my education in the pursuit of laughs, something which Mr Pellegrini took a very dim view of.

He didn't say, "Holland, you'll never amount to much."

But he might as well have done. And maybe he had a point.

Only two stars from the Daily Telegraph, albeit from a pretentious ass.

*

Take Thirteen ended with me recounting my Mr Chmai story to a packed Royal Albert Hall, an audience which included my old headmaster, Mr Anthony Pellegrini. Mr Pellegrini was an unusual man. Not very old, nor very big and yet he had a remarkable presence and a complete command over his staff and pupils. My school is a London comprehensive with an intake from a broad church and is best exemplified by two kids in my year. Both the sons of Irish immigrants; one went on to Oxford, became an accountant, married a doctor and his son went to Eton College. The other kid was as hard as nails, got expelled from school and promptly got himself seven years for armed robbery. Imagine then a typical rowdy and boisterous playground at lunchtime, and the whole space falling instantly silent the moment Mr Pellegrini appeared. His aura and control was a rare thing and even though he terrified me, he had a big bearing and influence on my life.

Since retiring, his presence might even have increased (depending on your viewpoint) with his becoming ordained to the priesthood. He officiated at my dad's funeral which felt completely fitting.

Standing on stage that evening at The Albert Hall, with Father Pellegrini front and centre, I was relieved to see him enjoying my speech. I wondered if he could recall the incident of shumbly blumbly and what he made of his ex-pupil now and his unorthodox choice of career. After the formalities we chatted and I didn't dare ask him. He congratulated me on my speech and I wonder if he knew how much this meant to me.

Take Seventeen

At the Third Stroke…

I like it when people make a go of things and particularly so in the arts with the ever-lengthening odds against being successful. Whenever I can, I like to be supportive but not always. A comedian friend of mine, who I hadn't seen for a long time, recently re-emerged from his comedy 'break', full of verve at having completed his first book.

A non-fiction book (easier than a novel?) on the theory of time, as in seconds, hours, days, weeks… A serious tome at just shy of eight hundred pages, I knew it would not be for me. Insufficient time, but I didn't say this.

A digest of his theory is that time does not exist and we should pay it no heed.

Immediately I thought of any number of scenarios…

"what do you mean, the plane has left? There is no such thing as 1300 hours. Here, read this excessively long book by my friend who is actually a comedian…"

Because night follows day, right? This is immutable and it always occurs in the same period of 'time' however it is measured. Similarly, the four seasons come and go and always in the same order and timeframe, most usually denoted as a year or twelve months or fifty something weeks...

As the years pass by, it is impossible (even for people with endless means and vanity) not to get smaller, greyer, fatter and more wrinkly until our time is eventually up.

Needless to say, I did not read his book but it did get me thinking about time. The great constant that answers to no one and never stops. Relentless. On and on. It never ceases.

That time passes too quickly is something we only appreciate too late in life. A reality that will resonate with my readers by varying degrees and largely dependent on their age. Middle-aged readers (and above) will nod sagely but young readers will be dismissive because they have all the time in the world, right?

As a young man I was interviewed for a job by a man who would become my boss. In our conversation it came up that he was forty-two and I recoiled. I felt so sorry that he had reached such a grand age and was still working. As I write this, I can barely remember being forty-two.

And although time is constant, there are relics associated with time denoting a bygone age and no better example is the speaking clock. Endless fun for kids the world over, listening over the telephone to the pips and the precise time...

"At the third stroke, it will be three o'clock p.m. precisely..."

An irony then that it is our mobile telephones which have rendered the speaking clock obsolete.

And yet, to my consternation and delight, I discovered that this service continues to this day. The telephone speaking clock remains. I know, who knew? And for whom?

This got me thinking about a modern day version of the same thing. A service which every contact in our phone address books will provide, albeit unwittingly. At least, they will if we call them at an ungodly hour...

Pick any contact at random in your phone and call them at say, 3 a.m. or thereabouts. You don't need to be precise or even know the time because they will tell you, although they might ask you first.

And they will answer their phone quickly as well.

"What are you calling for? Is everything okay?"

"Yes, everything is fine."

"Do you know what time it is? Why are you calling? It's three o'clock in the f**** morning. You scared the f**** shit out of me..."

The modern version of the speaking clock complete with colourful language.

But I like that the original phone service remains because I have an affection for anything from my past. Nostalgia. Another thing that younger readers won't appreciate (yet) and is the message of this short *Take*.

Time is constant and infinite but our allocation of it is not. Our time is finite and how much we each have is unknown.

This makes it precious and we waste it at our peril.

Take Eighteen

Coming Full Circle

Life came full circle for us with a recent trip to Leeds, the city where Nikki and I met at university many years ago.

It was not a reunion or even a hankering to return and reminisce over the place and time where Nikki managed to bag herself a husband of some pedigree. Or more realistically, the place and the time where I doggedly wore Nikki down and finally got her to see sense and give the funny little guy his shot.

No, the return to Leeds had a practical purpose, to show Paddy a course at the university that he might be interested in applying for.

With a train strike taking place, we set out in the dark at 6 a.m. for our meeting at noon with two stops along the way for the driver with an intemperate bladder. But as with everything I do, we arrived on time and waited outside a lecture theatre for various talks to begin.

My first time in a Leeds University lecture theatre in almost thirty years and old habits die hard because I promptly fell asleep.

Full on, head bobbing sleep much to Paddy's consternation. He prodded me repeatedly, perhaps to keep his chances of admission alive. No offence to the speakers but the theatre was warm, the lights were dimmed and that early start...

And to be fair it wasn't exactly riveting stuff.

During the subsequent tour, Nikki filled me in on what I'd slept through. Apparently, university is an opportunity for our young adults to learn life skills as well as a higher education.

Evidently, one previous student had decided to buy their entire supply of bread for a term all in one go. £250 on bread. It must have been chastening to watch it turn green. This is comic and tragic in equal measure but encouraging also because I adjusted upwards Paddy's chances of gaining a place.

Later, we visited our old university haunts and in particular a theatre that came to have such a bearing on my life.

Not a lecture theatre but a venue called the Riley Smith theatre, where I saw a comedian called Ben Elton in 1986 as mentioned in *Eclipsed*.

Ben remains a big comedy star in the UK filling theatres whenever he chooses to work as well as his canon of best-selling novels. That night in Leeds, he smashed the gig and rocked my world. I was unable to think of anything else but stand-up comedy and I wondered if I might be able to make a living in laughter. A lofty hope but some years later, Ben and I shared a bill at *The Royal Variety Performance* on BBC1 at the Dominion Theatre with Nikki in the front row, the mother of my three boys at the time.

The venue for that pivotal gig was bigger in my memory but much smaller now as I stood on the stage with Paddy and looked out at the void – the space I have spent my working life trying to fill with laughs.

Later, walking around the campus in the autumn drizzle, on plinths are faces of famous University alumni now prominent in business, the arts and sport. Their face, name, their subject and why they are noteworthy, and I shuddered, delighted not to have reached the fame threshold to be included.

It was odd to return to our old department. A beautiful building albeit no longer used as a teaching hub for all things textiles. And peculiar also that we should return with one of four sons. Our youngest. Someone we made together and who might now return to Leeds in his own right.

But not to study textiles, an industry which has long migrated East and taken its jobs with it. Not that textiles ever interested me as a career as I promptly took the plunge and followed Ben Elton's lead.

Paddy is not looking at textiles but art. You know, drawing and painting. Another thing I had no affinity for but I have always loved and admired. That said, there are many more starving artists than plump ones...

The chances of making a living as an artist are remote. But no matter the odds, I am backing and encouraging Paddy all the way.

Do your best and see what happens.

A parenting mantra I have used before and has borne much fruit to which anyone who has read *Eclipsed* can attest.

Take Nineteen

Self-Harm

You will understand why I did it though.

Imagine the scene. I am sixteen years old, waiting to see a man who is not keen to see me. Mr McMahon, a man with a big responsibility. A maths tutor, handsomely paid by my parents and charged with getting me through my maths O-level. I have failed twice already and the pressure is mounting. My dad is pessimistic and especially so when I assure him that this time, I am 110% confident of passing.

Sitting in Mr McMahon's home, under his stairs and waiting while he finishes up a lesson with some other dullard, I have strict instructions not to approach his tank which is opposite me.

Not a tank with a turret but a fish tank. A fish tank that was wildly exciting to an inquisitive and mischievous sixteen year old. Poised on its own plinth, illuminated and containing only one fish.

A piranha.

You can see my temptation now?

Mr McMahon was a gruff Irishman who did little to hide his disappointment in boys like me even though we paid his mortgage. A big man and suitably foreboding, his word was rarely defied.

But, come on, it's a f**** piranha fish.

His ongoing lesson still had ten minutes to run, so I had time and the necessary equipment. But what I hadn't accounted for, but I now understand only too well, was that Mr McMahon was a man of a certain age and one who drinks a lot of coffee, possibly to stay awake. This meant that he peed a lot. His frequent toilet breaks were difficult to predict but this was not enough to put me off.

Need I remind you, it's not a goldfish.

I had brought from home the necessary equipment to stab my thumb, my compass of course. What else is a compass for? I borrowed a chair from Mr McMahon's dining room to stand on to gain access to the lid of his tank. I duly stabbed my thumb and was squeezing blood into the water in the hope to see the fish go completely ape-shit.

Only it didn't.

It didn't do anything. WTF. Call yourself a piranha? My blood slowly dissipated throughout the tank, all around the fish and yet it hardly moved, unlike me when Mr McMahon suddenly appeared from his office and he duly went ape-shit.

Which brings me to another episode of aqua-based violence that was also my undoing when I enticed Paddy (youngest son) from his broadband lair with the prospect of watching *Jaws* with his old-man.

I made the classic error of being far too exuberant. The movie had rocked my world but would it do the same for Paddy?

Er, no.

And I have some sympathy with him because *Jaws* hasn't fared so well. Ironically, it has less teeth than I recall. But undeterred I demanded another movie night and this time I went for a film that could not possibly fail…

Misery.

I should say that its star, James Caan has some form in this area. When Tom was making *The Impossible* in Alicante (the tsunami wave sequence) he was ruled out of filming with an ear infection. Flitting back and forth as my gigs permitted, I arrived in Spain armed with a bunch of movies for us to bond over, including *Rollerball*, starring Caan, which I hyped out of all recognition. Barely twenty minutes in, Tom was asleep and I needed to reconcile how easily pleased I was in my childhood.

But *Misery* with Kathy Bates and James Caan is a big success. Not as well received as *The Shawshank Redemption* which we had already chalked off in lockdown (another Stephen King, so maybe *The Green Mile* beckons) but still a thumbs up.

You may recall, *Misery* is the story about a famous author trapped in hell and watching it this time around some parallels with my own life struck me.

Not that I am trapped in a house by a female psychopath…

What I mean is, that Caan's character endures great suffering for his writing. In this instance, unimaginable agony meted out by Kathy Bates with repeated compound fractures of both his legs. Awful to watch but surely his hurt is salved by his literary success? His book tours and general acclaim. Not to mention his sales and mighty riches…

In the movie we see him having survived his terrifying ordeal. Smartly dressed walking to a Manhattan restaurant for lunch with his agent, albeit with a limp and a cane, but so what?

As literary hurt goes, try enduring the pain of writing a book that no one reads. Stephen King doesn't know a thing about literary pain. Indeed, some unread authors might even snap their own legs if it means being invited to a Literary Festival and the chance to share a green room (marquee) with Joanna Trollope or Jonathan Franzen.

And finally, I did eventually pass my maths O-Level (grade C) and no one was more delighted than Mr McMahon because he would never have to see me again.

But I suspect that his Piranha missed me terribly.

Take Twenty

A Selfie Tale

As a youngster I used to daydream about becoming famous which I think (and hope) is a common infatuation. I didn't really know what for, a footballer most probably but it didn't matter, just as long as I was famous. What a glorious prospect, I imagined, to be recognised everywhere I went. So, when I fixated on comedy and I began to play the clubs, win awards and was invited on to television, it all seemed logical and according to plan.

So am I disappointed now that I am not Jerry Seinfeld?

No, not at all even though I did chuck everything at it. Maybe this is because of the internet (and social media) because being famous nowadays is so much more exposing.

Or it's because I am not burdened by an ego.

Recently, I headed into London to meet up with an old university friend. Waiting outside the pub, I became conscious of a young woman who had spotted me. It's a sixth sense I have developed over the years and it rarely fails me.

She began to cross the road in my direction. She looked highly anxious and I suspected I knew why. She uttered something quickly. Her voice was short for a lack of breath and I detected an accent. European but I didn't know from where. I caught only three words but they were key.

"…Tom Holland's dad."

At this, I nodded wryly or at least I thought I did. But I might have got this wrong because her anxiety heightened and this put me ill-at-ease also.

"Would you mind if I take a photo with you?"

She asked very politely but her voice continued to falter.

"…but only if it's okay. And I am very sorry to ask…"

Now it was me playing catch up.

If it's okay?

Of course it's okay. And it's understandable too. She is a fan of Tom (there are millions of them) and on a trip to London she happens to encounter the man who made him. Clearly, not all my own work. Nikki was ever-present and heavily involved and with a much greater hand in his career than mine, as readers of *Eclipsed* will know.

And what harm to take a photo with a young fan?

The selfie is the new autograph. Proof of an encounter to share with her friends in possibly France, but more likely somewhere further east and north. Maybe Scandinavia. I would like to ask her because I am interested but I don't of course. Not these days.

In my newish role and public position of being 'Tom Holland's dad' I feel a certain responsibility not be to be aloof or unpleasant and this is not an onerous task for me you will be happy to read.

Of course, it's no trouble. I'm Tom's dad. I get it. I smile and try to assure her but she still seemed anxious at her 'imposition'.

"I really love…" She began.

At this I nodded knowingly, not to be dismissive but because people regularly profess their love for Tom and now I am inured to it. Practically every parent I meet has a child who is Tom's number one fan. But like half the novels on sale at an airport, they can't all be No.1 bestsellers.

And with us both dithering on a London street, I was keen to take the photo to put this young lady out of her misery. But then everything changes.

"…your books."

I turned to look at her.

My books!

You love my books? Please, note the use of the plural here. I certainly did. It rendered me even more obliging and my smile didn't need to be forced. She loves my books! My two brothers have only managed one book of mine between them and this stranger had read at least two.

Of course this might have been a ploy on her part. A compliment to soften me up. No doubt, she loves Tom also and found my books through him, which is perfectly fine because writers just want to be read.

So my thanks to the young lady in a side street between the Strand and Covent Garden. As a fan of my book(s) there is a high probability that she might read this *Take*.

It will be a fun read for her to know that she has revived and massaged my dormant ego and has made me realise what glories might have been.

I end on a quick note to anyone else who might encounter me unexpectedly...

By all means, do say hello. Selfies are available if you wish, but do perhaps learn one thing from this *Take* – that my ego is alive and needy after all and praising my books ahead of any such request makes eminent sense.

Just saying.

Take Twenty-One

Flower Power

People tend to avoid stressful situations, although not always. Free divers leap into view, literally. People who fling themselves off buildings or mountains, staking their lives on a sliver of nylon and all for kicks and clicks. Such daredevils need continually to up the ante which poses an ethical question for those online voyeurs, are they complicit in their eventual splat?

Other occasions are less risky but no less stressful and yet we continue on with them.

That dinner parties were banned in lockdown was one of the few upsides of Covid 19 – because throwing a dinner party can be pure stress and particularly when guests deviate from the usual bottle of wine as their arrival offering. Wine is so easily received and dealt with, plus it can come in useful if guests are more thirsty than the host has budgeted for.

But flowers as a gift are much less welcome.

Don't get me wrong, I like flowers. Who doesn't like flowers?

Flowers are beautiful and fragrant. The pungent aroma of lilies always lifts the spirits. But I don't always like to receive flowers. Like when I have things in the oven that shouldn't be or things that need to be in the fridge but aren't and now I am in receipt of something that needs to be in water.

They could be left in a bucket I suppose but isn't this rude? And leaving the flowers in their little pouch of water isn't much of an option either.

"Nikki, where are the vases?"

There is something peculiar about a gift that the recipient is charged with keeping alive.

"…the vases. Where do we keep the vases?"

"I don't fucking know. Check the cupboards. Shall I take the meat out?"

We have vases. I know we have vases but can I find them? Where could the vases have gone? Vases are not like scissors which are useful elsewhere in the house and so could be anywhere…

None of our boys are likely to ever commandeer a vase.

And it has to be the right vase. Size and style appropriate. Not too big or else the flowers are lost or too small so the flowers can't breathe…

Speaking of scissors, the wrapping needs to come off: yards of unnecessary cellophane and paper that will fill up the bin. And not forgetting the pesky plant food sachet.

I am happy to feed our guests but I should not have to feed their gifts.

And so to dinner which passes off as planned and hoped for. The booze doesn't run out, most of the food is eaten. Compliments to the chef are proffered. No tears and some laughs too. Contentious subjects avoided and arguments swerved.

And finally, thank the Lord, the event winds down with one couple initiating the first move for the exit. Eye contact with a spouse and the mention of an Uber and an early start the next day. A football match, perhaps? Coats are retrieved. Keys and phones are gathered and finally the front door snaps shut and the optional pre-bed clear up can begin. Cooking pots filled to soak overnight, maybe a dishwasher cycle begins and leftovers of perishable food are covered in clingfilm and put into the fridge, to be thrown out days later.

The guests have gone but their flowers remain, wilting and dying before my eyes. Over the coming days, the water reduces and changes colour. Petals first droop, then drop. So does the pollen which can stain anything it encounters. And eventually a pong sets in, before the final task of disposal.

Flowers are not a gift.

Receiving flowers is being given a chore.

Unless they are dried flowers and then I get it. Flowers are like apricots. They're much better dried.

So choose your gifts carefully and if you are ever invited to Chez Holland for dinner – a bottle of wine is ample.

Take Twenty-Two

University Blues

Like most people of advancing years, I hanker for the past. The good old days when things were better than they are now. This is a cliché of course but concerning the UK comedy scene it happens to be true. I am fortunate that I was there to enjoy it and that I happened to be peaking in those halcyon days.

By peaking, I mean that I had made the hallowed grade of topping the bill. The headliner. The closer. The last act. The funniest act.

We've saved the best 'til last!

No, pressure then…

And for no extra money I might add. Just the glory.

Hmm.

A glorious time for comedians because the clubs were packed to the gunnels.

I recall one Friday evening particularly vividly. I was booked to perform two shows (doubling-up) – not uncommon for in vogue acts on a booming circuit.

I opened a show at the Newbury Corn Exchange (West of London) and then I drove further west to close a show at a comedy club called *Jesters* in Bristol.

As soon as I arrived at *Jesters*, my earlier triumph at Newbury (darling) was forgotten. I had a new task in hand and immediately I sensed that something was awry.

I arrived during the final interval. The club was packed and I learned that the previous acts had all crashed and burned. If the promoter was pleased to see me then he hid it well.

It transpired that the gig had been ruined by two rival factions; students of Bristol University pitted against students from the University of Western England and I suspected that any antagonism probably hinged on snobbery.

England is well known for its class structure and this is best demonstrated with our elite schools and universities.

America has the Ivy League. We have the Russel Group where the 'brightest' and certainly the most privileged kids attend.

Bristol University is one of the elite with a large contingent of its intake hailing from expensive private schools. The University of Western England is more bog standard with an intake of more ordinary kids.

The promoter was desperate. Already, some punters (the few non-students) had asked for refunds and everything hinged on his headline act.

"Dom, I really need you to pull this out of the bag…"

No pressure, then…

The compere (MC) had no desire to prolong his agony and glumly explained to me in our green room…

'Dom, they're a nightmare, I'm just gonna get you straight on. Good luck.'

On hearing my name and making my way to the stage to hardly any applause from the disgruntled room, it suddenly struck me. The angle I needed to possibly pull this gig around. The very thing that I needed to say. A risk certainly, but it felt like my only option.

On stage, I grabbed the microphone and said very little, preferring to front out the audience's indifference with the bickering and goading between the two factions continuing. And given this new 'angle' of mine, this rather suited me. I needed to be patient. Timing would be critical and so I waited for hostilities to eventually abate.

Finally, the shushes and appeals prevailed and a temporary window presented itself to me and by now I was ready.

"Okay, before I start… I just need to flag up what's been occurring here this evening. I'm told that we have something of a rivalry going on here this evening…

So, on the count of three… I would like all the students from the West of England University to give me a cheer…"

And cheer they did. A guttural proletarian war cry of a cheer amidst the predictable boos from their loftier opponents.

At this, I expect the promoter had his head in his hands, but he didn't know that there was method in my madness.

Again, I patiently waited for the noise to quell, whereupon I continued…

"…and on the count of three… if I could have a cheer please from the students of Bristol University…"

And cheer they did.

A much more patrician cheer, laden with pomp and derision. It was reminiscent of the House of Commons, with the posh Conservatives waving their order papers and goading the working class benches opposite.

And while this played out, again I paused, like a patient angler waiting for a once in a lifetime trout.

Silence eventually fell and now was my time…

"…only because last night… I did a gig at Cambridge University, which is where you lot wanted to go, but didn't get in."

There followed a moment in time of complete silence as my barb registered with everyone present before it broke into an almighty roar of unifying laughter. I suspect that the Bristol University students got this a little quicker but the opposition were not too far behind.

A slight at the elite students and pricking their pomposity since it happens to be true and with it, a uniting laugh as all students were reconciled and became ONE. The thrust being that everything is relative and aren't we all rejects in one form or other?

I had one of the best club sets of my life. Refunds were forgotten. I had saved the gig.

But for the same money as everyone else…

Go figure.

Take Twenty-Three

We're Gonna Need a Different Excursion

The movie, *Jaws* had a big impact on me as you know from *Take Nineteen*. It kept me awake for weeks and any prospect of getting into water with sharks was completely impossible.

But when in South Africa… and of course, much has changed in the intervening forty years. I am an adult now. A dad to four boys and my youngest was in Cape Town filming a TV show and I got to tag along.

My first trip to Cape Town, a beautiful city which puts many of the European coastal cities in the shade. South Africa is a unique country in so far as everyone knows at least something about its history. Official segregation is over and yet its legacy still lingers with an unofficial hierarchy of 'blacks', 'coloureds' (Asians) and then 'whites' (their terms by the way, not mine). So it is awkward that the most feared beast in the country happens to be called the Great White.

And one of the go-to Cape Town excursions is the dubious opportunity to get in the water with these apex predators.

Nikki immediately ruled herself out even after I explained that we would be in cages. And a big cage too, specifically designed to keep wealthy and all-important tourists from being eaten.

"No way. Not a chance."

I on the other hand remained game which is an unfortunate expression. But really, what harm could come to me? Thousands of tourists have done this already and all of them have survived.

I'm in and all ears for the man explaining the shark swimming experience to me.

The sharks are wild, obviously. There is no great white shark in captivity and rightly so. And being wild animals, naturally a boat is required.

I'm not great with boats. I prefer to look at them than be on them because I am prone to sea sickness. But I can make an exception in certain circumstances, like being in South Africa and with the opportunity to be in the habitat of the world's most feared animal.

But then he mentions the temperature of the ocean bordering South Africa. Freezing all year round, given it originates from the Antarctic Ocean a few thousand miles south.

I'm not great with cold.

I don't do cold showers even though I am aware of the health benefits. I'm not even terribly fond of heated swimming pools.

I prefer to look at water than be in it, unless it's a bath.

But again I can make an exception. Of course I can. This is a unique opportunity and I can suffer a freezing ocean for the chance to see Jaws up close and personal.

"..and because of the cold, you have to wear wet suits…"

Now he really has my attention because… I'm not great with wet suits.

Call me fussy but I like my clothes to be dry. I don't like clothes that are exhausting to put on. Wet clothes should be pulled off, not pulled on. And it seems to me that wet suits are always wet because of prior use and this presents obvious hygiene issues.

"…and you will need to wear a complete wet suit."

Hmm…

"What is a complete wet suit?" I ask.

You know, a full suit. Long legs and arms. Plus hat, gloves and shoes.

Now I am rapidly shifting my position.

I'm not great with dubious hygiene. Wet suits are wet because they have been worn already by someone else. And how do you think the previous occupiers warm themselves in a freezing ocean? I am being asked to squeeze into a suit that someone else has just pissed in.

And given that these suits permit people to frolic with man-eating sharks, I wonder if urine is the only bodily excretion these suits are exposed to.

The man-eating shark I could handle. But another tourist's bodily fluids is a step too far.

"No thanks. I'm out."

Take Twenty-Four

Dear God

In stand-up comedy it is advisable to avoid subjects that split an audience in half. Contentious subjects like politics and any inflammatory societal issues that tend to wreak havoc.

And religion of course.

In my pursuit of laughs, I like to plough a much safer furrow. I prefer the anomalies of life: like my toaster and why I am always inclined to pop up the bread too early.

Stand-up is difficult enough without alienating people and that's why I admire the comedians brave enough and clever enough to plot such an uphill route.

The same applies to writing this book. Stick to toasters and leave the thorny issues to more skilled and learned thinkers.

But with that said...

Religion.

I thought of spirituality recently whilst attending a funeral which I am afraid are becoming more frequent occasions at my time of life.

Naturally, funerals are sombre affairs but there are degrees of sadness, depending on circumstances. A funeral of a very old person (a good innings) is less sad than a funeral for a life cut short, but even in these circumstances there are still levels of grief, as was the case at this funeral for a young man called Oliver, who was only thirty-two.

Oliver had been born with a fatal and untreatable disease, so his death hadn't come as a shock and might even have been a relief given that his excruciating and continual pain was finally over. Furthermore, the overwhelming feeling at his funeral was not grief but admiration for Oliver's fortitude in how he had lived his very challenging life.

It is not easy to helm a funeral, to find the right words and tone. This celebrant had a warm demeanour and I think he did well. He smiled frequently. He spoke affectionately and he talked about God and his place and plans for Oliver.

But outside the crematorium a fellow mourner was much less impressed than me. He complained bitterly about the disease (a fair point) and he questioned the presence of any God who would allow such a condition to exist. A frequent conundrum for everyone to ponder and wrestle with.

Religion has played a prominent role in my upbringing and life. Attending mass every Sunday (plus feast days) and all the beats and landmarks of Catholic life; First Holy Communion, Confirmation, Confession, Marriage… have all informed my life as a boy and later as an adult and a parent.

Now I would describe my faith as more habitual than live,

although I do like the idea of a God and something bigger and better than us. And a place for good people as well when their time on Earth is up. But do I truly believe in something as binary as Heaven and Hell? I am not so sure. But no matter, since I like being part of a church. I like the belonging and the sense of community.

Four of my aunts were nuns. Kinder people I have never met, working in Africa and India and devoting their lives to others. I happen to be writing this *Take* in Cape Town in a plush hotel and nothing like the aids hostel that my aunt founded and built in her retirement, which survives her and still operates today. Her name was Sister Bernard (Breda was her real name) and I am very proud of her life and her legacy.

I enjoy the calm and the rhythm of a church service. Going to mass punctuates my week. I appreciate its cadence and structure. It's not so long. Never more than an hour or else the place would be even more empty. I also like the quiet. A time to pause and reflect. I usually concentrate on what I have and how fortunate I am. And I don't mean my relative wealth against the three billion people still confined to life on a dollar a day. That everyone living in the West are amongst the wealthiest human beings who have ever lived on Earth is a chastening fact.

I concentrate on more basic human things to be grateful for. My good health and that I don't suffer with the disease that so cruelly dispatched young Oliver. A quirk of his parents' genes that they knew nothing about until Oliver was born and all of their lives were irrevocably altered.

And what do I pray for?

Well, the obvious, I suppose. For any friends or people I know who happen to be ill, that they might be granted a reprieve.

But mostly I pray to say thank you to my God and yours for what I have and also if I am being perfectly candid, I pray to ask…

…for just a little bit more!

*

To add…

Years ago I was speaking at an infamous boozy lunch at *The Grosvenor House Hotel* on Park Lane in London. A thousand property types who I was charged with entertaining, which I duly did and why I was invited back the following year. After my second appearance, a businessman (present at both) requested a meeting with me at his office. We talked about everything and anything including our similar backgrounds and upbringing. I must have mentioned my aunt and her plans to build an AIDS hostel in South Africa. He had made his considerable fortune building retail superstores in the UK but perhaps his most important building might be the simple AIDS hostel and orphanage he completely funded in Cape Town.

Of course, my tearful aunt, Sister Bernard called his generosity the work of God and this is fine.

And who knows, maybe it was.

Take Twenty-Five

Don't Try This at Home

Things we watch on television often look easy and none more so than the game of snooker.

Think pool only bigger and with more balls, which sounds like a euphemism but isn't.

Snooker is a mesmeric game to watch but only when played by players with sufficient skills. Watching a snooker maestro plot his way around the immaculate table with diminishing numbers of balls is transfixing. The brilliant green table and the shiny multi-coloured balls. The myriad camera angles with some balls dropping delicately into pockets and others rocketing home. The reds never to be seen again, the colours coming back for more until the hallowed and most valuable black ball is all alone.

And everything at the behest of the all-powerful cue ball. The only white ball on the table has complete control which might be an unfortunate metaphor for our Identitarian times.

But leaving aside any unintentional undertones, we can agree that snooker is a beguiling watch and I wonder how many viewers are encouraged to pick up a snooker cue themselves and the rude awakening that awaits them.

The size of the table to begin with.

"…but it looks so much smaller on the telly."

And then to the game itself which is fiendishly difficult. A sport of millimetres and less. Unfairly maligned for the reddened faces and the paunches of its star players but this is a mistake and is usually just ugly classism.

Because snooker is a display of physics, mechanics and precision geometry combined with guile, surgical planning and steel-like nerve.

On television, a game of professional snooker (known as a frame) is a thing of beauty and wonder. Some frames are completed in a matter of minutes and others can stretch to more than an hour.

Two players duelling but never touching. A hybrid of chess and poker with sublime physical skill, tactics and nerve. It is fascinating and why millions of people around the world tune in to watch.

But snooker played by occasional players is impossible to watch. Typically frames are excessively long. Like Monopoly, it is a game more likely to be abandoned than completed.

The World Championship Snooker final is played over thirty-five frames.

Ordinary Joes playing thirty-five frames of snooker might not live long enough to complete such a match.

Best left to the professionals then which is something that equally applies to stand-up comedy.

Done well, stand-up comedy appears to be easy. The timing and the cadence of a seasoned stand-up, so in sync with an audience that the pauses are part of the art. A microphone in the right hands is all that is needed to regale a full theatre for hours on end. A successful comedy film is qualified by two or three laugh out loud moments. The laugh count of a stand-up over ninety-minutes runs into hundreds. Stand-up comedy done well is a beautiful thing. Woody Allen with his moose, Brian Regan in the emergency room, Sebastian Maniscalco on his way to see Hamilton, Kathleen Madigan, Jerry Seinfeld...

But stand-up in less capable hands...

Even with the addition of laugh tracks, fake cutaways and the skills of a television editor, no one is fooled. Bad stand-up is like a geared car being driven for the first time by a learner. It moves forward but not as it should. The audience waits patiently for the next comedian who is hopefully funny, which is the one and only requirement to be a professional stand-up comedian.

Take Twenty-Six

The Weird Uncle

During my long career (ongoing?) in comedy I have observed many tropes used by comedians, one of which is the embarrassing older relative. Always a man and usually an uncle. A man who is unlikely to risk his computer ever being fixed. He lives alone, he often smells and he is usually only tolerated or seen at weddings and funerals.

It's a trope commonly used by Irish comics and although I understand it well enough it was never something I related to. I hail from a very large family. My mum is one of twelve, my dad is one of five and despite so many uncles to choose from, none of them fitted this mould thereby curtailing my comedy options.

My nieces and nephews have all grown up. One is about to become a doctor, no less. But courtesy of my youngest brother and his late arrival to breeding, I am grateful to have a young nephew again (just five years old) as a kind of precursor to my next landmark life phase, becoming a grandfather.

I was a very tactile dad. Playfights galore and a relentless penchant for tickling. An irrepressible need to tease and antagonise, all bounded by a set of unusual and made-up vocabulary. You may recall shumbly blumbly. The following terms will make sense only to my four sons but I list them here to illustrate my point:

The Itsy Bitsys, Lotus, C'tanga, Nam, Trust Me Zones (TMZees), the Butchers, Hand Wobbles (on the bed), Skiing (bed again), the Back Balance, the Squeezes: soft, medium and hard, the Crunch Punch, the Tree Climb... on and on it went with me chucking my boys about beds and lounges until they became too heavy. This continues today with my young nephew although he is much more circumspect about the whole thing.

On the day of the Queen's funeral, we hosted a bunch of my family, young nephew included, to watch the service and have sandwiches and a cream tea. How very English and proper. And a popular idea it seemed, given the scarcity of clotted cream in the run up to the sombre day.

The funeral was a great send-off and experience. The sun shone in London and everything passed off as it should.

I have written before in *Takes Vol. 1* about my need for comfort. I am a committed pyjama man. In winter, I go complete winceyette suit - full length trousers, jacket, all tucked in. I am a dedicated wearer of slippers with at least three pairs on the go so that I am never without fur on foot. That said, with a dog, a large house and being absent-minded, there are still occasions when I might need to squeeze into a pair of Nikki's.

As was the case on the day of the funeral. As my brother and sister (plus Granny Tess) were leaving, I was outside our house in Nikki's slippers as they packed up their cars.

Some slippers are unisex of course but not this pair.

As cars drove by, I daresay some attention was drawn to my odd appearance, not that I noticed or cared.

Until I clocked the look on Paddy's face. My youngest son looked mortified that his dad should be cuddling a five year old child whilst wearing shorts and a pair of fluffy slippers. He was probably terrified that someone he knows from school might drive past.

"…you're the weird uncle." He spat under his breath.

If this was an insult then it did not land. Instead, I roared with laughter but on reflection it did cause me some hurt.

Because for years, I've been watching comedians getting easy laughs with the weird uncle schtick and all this time there was a weird uncle in my family after all.

The wood for the trees… as the expression goes.

All along, I have been the weird uncle!

To think of the laughs I have forfeited. If I'd only known this on the way up. It might have made all the difference. I might have even made it.

Damn it.

Take Twenty-Seven

Innocent Until Proven Guilty

One of the glories of being a comedian is meeting such colourful and eclectic characters over the years. From the very famous to the unknowns, an array of people I would never have met had I opted for a more traditional way of earning a crust.

Talented types (in the main) but also quirky and most with evident foibles. Many have depended on various crutches (substances) and sadly some who are no longer with us and creating laughs.

One such character is Jeff Innocent, a comedian making much hay of late enjoying a beautiful swansong in his career and life. One of the most sought after live acts on the circuit, having recently been voted the UK's Best Comedian and good for him.

Jeff is easy to imagine. Picture a 1970's cockney football hooligan complete with tracksuit, skinhead and earrings you could hang curtains from and you've got Jeff. A tall and menacing presence, anyone encountering him is likely to jump to the wrong conclusion that he's an old-school racist and a man best avoided.

Only this would be flat wrong. His wife is from Ghana and provides him with his funniest anecdotes and material. A perfect marriage then?

I introduce Jeff here because the story I am about to recount is his. A true tale. It happened to Jeff and because it happens to be funny, poignant and painful, I asked his permission to share it with the world.

Thankfully he agreed.

*

One Sunday, Jeff was out for a drive with his young son on their way home. The sun was still shining in the late afternoon and the country lanes in the East London/Essex borders were quiet with no other traffic and little happening on either side of the hedge-rowed lanes. Passing through an occasional village boasting enormous houses with wrought iron gates and long connecting drives. The sort of drums popular with West Ham and Tottenham Hotspur football players.

Nothing really to draw the eye until Jeff rounded a shallow bend and there in the distance was a man walking towards him holding a petrol can. Clearly, a stranded motorist and with nothing particularly pressing, the mood caught Jeff and he duly slowed his car to a stop.

The man was frantic and mightily relieved as Jeff lowered his window for the stricken motorist. He had indeed run out of petrol. He hadn't seen another car for ages and getting desperate had decided to walk in the hope of finding a garage.

The nearest garage was about five miles away and being the good egg that he is, Jeff decided to give him a lift to and fro.

The man was hugely grateful. Clutching his petrol can, he clambered into Jeff's car for the ten mile round trip. A short enough journey but it might have felt longer for Jeff with the motorist lavishing his thanks and explaining endlessly how he had come to be stranded. His phone had died, so he used Jeff's mobile to call his wife with the good news that a Samaritan had rescued him.

Jeff isn't one for fuss and no doubt he was delighted finally to see the garage ahead. The chap filled his can and purchased an array of chocolates and other goodies as a thank you and also insisted on giving Jeff's son a ten pound note.

Back on the road, the thank yous started again and I would not be surprised if the inbound journey was quicker than the outbound.

By the time they arrived back at his car, the man was tearful with joy. Standing on the roadside, he might have even gone in for a hug but this would have been a mistake. Jeff is not a hugger. And they would not have swapped phone numbers either.

For Jeff, driving off with the man waving in his rear view mirror, I daresay he felt warm and fuzzy at his good deed. Saving a chap from possibly having to sleep in his car with his panicking wife in the dark also.

Jeff would have enjoyed sharing this tale with his wife, Kareema and no doubt he slept well that night. Lying in his warm bed, he probably imagined the chap eventually getting home and telling his wife about the rough looking Guardian Angel who had come to his rescue.

The next morning, Jeff had a few errands to run and he needed to retrieve something from his car.

Still early with a cold bite to the air, Jeff opened his trunk and peered inside.

And what did he see?

The man's petrol can, full of fuel, but in his sheer excitement, he had left it in Jeff's car.

Take Twenty-Eight

The Colour Purple

With his kind permission, I frame this *Take* with one of my favourite circuit jokes. Kevin Day was already a heavyweight stand-up when I took my comedy plunge. A wordsmith comedian who didn't feel the need to shout and scream, which is all the rage nowadays and perhaps why I liked his craft so much. Like me, Kevin is a Londoner with Irish heritage although of grittier stock, which he might thank me for flagging and is relevant for his brilliant joke...

"...I got reviewed the other day by the Guardian...

Kevin Day, the middle class comedian...

It was a good review but I was furious. Middle Class! Me. I'm not middle-class. I was explaining this just the other day to my cleaner..."

*

I don't pay much attention to what I wear. Certainly, the colour of my clothes is unimportant and comes a long way behind comfort. This is a big mistake according to Nikki who happens to be very fashion confident. Strident even, although I use this word cautiously. Let's just say that Nikki is sufficiently assured to know what suits me and is forthright in sharing her insights.

And often her 'advice' is based on colour alone. Colour is a big thing for Nikki because she has had her colours done and I don't mean her roots.

Nikki has seen a qualified colour consultant. A 'professional' who is expert on what colours suit individuals, categorising people by the seasons: Autumn, Winter, Spring and Summer.

I have not had my colours done because I do not have sufficient time left on Earth to waste it on such nonsense.

One garment of mine that fell foul of Nikki's approval is a zip-up hooded sweat top. Comfortable and warm, easy-on, easy-off, what's not to like? Well, apparently the colour – burgundy, which doesn't suit me, and why unbeknownst to me, it was donated to a local charity shop. I now understand that Nikki does this regularly but up until this instance, I had put my missing clothes down to a busy house and an ad hoc laundry system.

Dirty clothes accumulate in individual bedrooms. Then they combine on the ground floor, process through the washing machine and then either the tumble dryer or more likely an array of airing frames, radiators and balustrades… throughout the ground floor and garden (my preferred option). Post ironing, the chances of a laundered garment returning to the correct wardrobe is practically nil.

Which brings me to an incident concerning my hoodie and a couple of young cleaners.

I am not a fan of cleaners, not for any ideological reasons but because in my view, they begin well, but then they become comfortable and quickly fade. Also, I am often home when they 'clean' and I worry they might think I'm a loser without a job.

Plus the annoying need to clear up ahead of their arrival and the stress that begins as soon as they leave and the house looks good - but for how long?

This cleaning duo were giggling teenagers who supplemented their wages by rifling my boys money stashes. Sam flagged this early on and they kept on finding it as he secreted it elsewhere.

I should have dispatched them there and then but I don't like confrontation and being on TV at the time, I figured I could afford such petty pilfering. And yet their fate would be sealed all because of my hoodie.

One morning, being chased from room to room with my laptop, exiting as the cleaning duo hoovered because I can't write and hover my legs (insufficient core), I saw my hoodie hanging on our newel post and I quickly pulled it on. I noticed this particular morning that they were especially giggly and although I couldn't understand them, it seemed their hilarity was directed at me.

Things became clear when Nikki returned home and looked at me aghast.

"Where did you get that hoodie from?"

In our quick exchange, Nikki's charitable unilateral donations were exposed, which was galling but not as unsettling as, so whose hoodie was I wearing?

This explains the cleaners delight. Not only does the wastrel man of this house not work but he also wears our clothes.

There could be no coming back from such ignominy. I like people laughing at me but only on my terms. They were gone and we never saw them again.

A mutual parting of the ways if ever there was one.

Take Twenty-Nine

...and I Will Make You Laugh

The Bible tells us that the meek shall inherit the Earth. This is a kindly notion and might well provide some solace for the meek. Something to look forward to, but only for the meek who believe in the Bible.

A phrase not in the Bible but is wise and has more provenance is...

Those with the highest skills have the fullest bellies.

Meaning, the most skilled people earn the most money and are able to enjoy more of life's luxuries.

A career is essentially the commercialisation of skills. Skills that we have acquired through training but occasionally through God-given gifts.

This is the essence of education. To acquire skills which can be deployed in exchange for money. And the more rarefied our skills, the more we are able to charge.

A paediatric neurosurgeon is the most skilled person in a hospital.

Much more skilled than the porter who wheels the patient down for surgery and even more skilled than fellow surgeons from different specialities. The paediatric neurosurgeon trumps the orthopaedic surgeon. The brain being complex (and more important?) than the knee… and a child is more valued and emotive than an old person with a wonky hip.

But too often, careers are assessed on income alone. This is understandable because money is an easy metric to audit but it is not always an accurate reflection of the skills rendered and the value proffered. It must be galling for the fine artist who can produce a beautiful portrait but who struggles to make a living in comparison to the 'star' modern artists who can barely paint but earn fortunes. Engineers also. It seems to me that the clever people responsible for a bridge that spans a river (not to mention the builders who install it) or a new tunnel beneath a metropolis are much more skilled than the lawyers and bankers who put the deal together and yet who do you think gets a larger slice of the pie?

Because some skills, even though they are greatly admired, do not command commensurate remuneration.

Like being able to kill people.

Hear me out.

Leaving aside assassins (James Bond types) who are presumably well paid, but what about the tough guy who remains standing after a bar brawl?

Tough guys get our admiration but I reckon not the cash they deserve.

I mean men like Bryan Mills.

There is much to admire about Bryan. A man who loves his daughter above everything else and he demonstrates with aplomb.

All decent dads feel this same affection but few have such commitment and even fewer have the requisite skills.

Bryan is man in possession of a very particular set of skills, acquired over a very long career. Skills that make Bryan a nightmare for people and particularly those in the sex trade who have the temerity to abduct his daughter from a Paris apartment. A bad choice as Bryan calls upon the skills which all men (most men?) daydream of having.

Bryan is expert at communications and technology. He is highly intelligent. He is a magnificent driver. He doesn't need to sleep. And there's one more thing…

Oh yes.

Bryan can kick the living shit out of any number of incoming assailants.

Plus he has a neat way with words, coining the immortal phrase…

"I will look for you. I will find you. And I will kill you."

Just to be able to say such a thing is the stuff of dad fantasy, let alone seeing it through.

But Bryan sets a very high bar. Too high for ordinary dads and a failing which got me to thinking about my own particular set of skills…

Skills I have acquired over a very long (ongoing?) career. Skills that are funny in nature both in the spoken and written word. At the very least, I can create smiles which is all well and good. Comedy is good for the soul and it has been good to me. Laughs rendered have clothed and fed the Holland family. Humour is admired. It can make people more attractive and popular. Some comedians play stadia nowadays, earning as much as rock stars.

And yet for all the wealth of the world's greatest comic, whoever this might be…

The credibility and skills of the comedian pale against men like Bryan Mills.

…I will look for you. I will find you… and I will make you laugh.

Just doesn't cut it.

But such a tendency towards violence is problematic because the Bible also instructs us not to kill.

Thou shalt not kill is one of the cardinal sins, ranking high in the Top Ten of transgressions and this is bad news for men like Bryan.

But the Bible also explains that there is no place in heaven for the rich man and this is problematic also because as explained in *Take Eleven*, Craft Work – everyone reading this book is comparatively rich.

Therefore, I expect that heavenly admissions will be dealt with on a case-by-case basis with certain dispensations for men like Bryan, with enormous kill counts but in very specific circumstances. However, I suspect such a broad licence will not apply to the rich man who happens to own a gas field or a new digital currency.

And maybe this is why some super wealthy individuals are on record to give up their entire fortunes during their lifetime. A place in heaven and everlasting life being the ultimate luxury purchase.

A huge gamble of course and perhaps one which should exercise us all.

Take Thirty

Cherry Pye

Growing up, it would never have occurred to me, that one day I would shop at *Cherry Pye* and in such unusual circumstances.

An infamous shop close to my home, selling all things naughty and erotic, its large window display festooned with lingerie, saucy adult outfits and a range of adult toys which drew the eye of every passing schoolboy.

In the window were fluffy handcuffs and whips and I expect within the store an array of more practical adult toys. The invasive kind? But it was more of a novelty shop than brazen sex shop which probably explains why its garish window display was permitted. And so, it remained for decades until just recently giving way to the developers to build more 'luxury' rabbit hutches. *Cherry Pye* had provided a noble service to the good people of Ealing in spicing up marriages and possibly staving off divorce lawyers. I noted with some delight that it remained open during lockdown, presumably under the essential service ruse. It's a confident individual who demands their right to buy a spanking paddle.

But why I am telling you all of this?

Well…

Some years ago, I was producing a short film based on the incident described in *Take Twenty-Seven, Innocent, Until Proven Guilty*.

A story too funny not to be filmed is how I sold it to Jeff. He was happy to play himself and he was joined by fellow comedian, Hal Cruttenden playing the stranded motorist with my son, Harry completing the venerable cast. Oh, and with Tom directing and paying for the whole thing.

A folly as it transpired because with the movie almost in the can (and where it would sadly remain) we had one final shot to complete our Oscar contending short-film – the reveal of Jeff opening his trunk and seeing the petrol can.

For this crucial shot, we had commandeered the beautiful house of a friend along with their vintage Jaguar car. My more modest house and Honda FRV (at the time) was not the look we needed.

The shot was as follows…

EXT. MANSION. MORNING

Front door opens. JEFF appears and goes to his car. Pops the trunk, sees the petrol can and looks suitably aghast.

Not that Jeff is not a fine actor, but it was decided that it might help if we put something in the trunk to genuinely surprise our leading man and give us the look we needed.

Brilliant. But what to leave in the trunk?

Nothing that would scare him or make him jump. We went

through lots of suggestions – all rejected – until someone suggested a sex toy.

Brilliant.

I explained that Mr. and Mrs. H didn't have any such thing, so an item would need to be purchased and unsurprisingly, no one was very keen to do so.

Then one evening, with all six Hollands driving home from Sunday lunch at my parent's house, sitting in traffic, Cherry Pye was ahead, open for business and I wondered. We had a quick conflab in the car. We confirmed that the required sex toy had not been purchased and so here was a golden opportunity.

But who was going to buy it?

Not me because I was driving the car (lame) and not Tom because he was likely to be recognised. And not Paddy because he was eight and they would likely have an age restriction on such purchases. This left Harry, Sam and Nikki. Harry emerged as everyone's preferred candidate but he was only thirteen and also the age threshold to buy a dildo. This brought a very reluctant Nikki into play. She agreed but was adamant that she would not go alone. Quickly, I suggested that Harry accompany her, without considering the implications of a mother and son shopping together in a sex emporium.

Delighted to be driving, I handed Nikki my wallet.

"Pay with cash."

I didn't relish explaining such a purchase to my accountants when my tax return is due.

Nikki and Harry disappeared into the shop that had beguiled

me as a child.

What happened next is the truth and cannot easily be explained…

In the shop, Nikki was mortified by the array of 'toys' available. Who knew? Some are enormous and her husband might have some explaining to do. It was an awkward browsing experience because they are somehow very obviously a mum and her son. No doubt, the proprietor had seen all sorts over the years and is rarely surprised, but this might just be a first…

Nikki grabbed a vibrator and made for the till with her head bowed. At the checkout she felt the need to explain herself and in doing so, she got it very wrong indeed…

"It's not what you think. It's for a film. My husband is making a film with my son."

A first surely?

Nikki and Harry emerged from the shop in wild hysterics. They jumped in the car like a couple of bank robbers and I stepped on the gas.

We got the shot we needed. If only the laptop with the footage hadn't been stolen in a house burglary, who knows what might have been. I felt terrible and apologised profusely to Jeff but at least now, his story has been immortalised in this book.

And finally, just to say that the 'toy' acquired as a prop was not kept by the Holland household.

Not needed!

And as you can imagine, it was not taken to a charity shop either.

Take Thirty-One

Farewell and Thank You

Aside from the people who work there and the very frequent flyers, for the rest of us, airports are comparatively exciting places. As transport hubs go at least. More exciting than train stations (warmer?) and definitely more alluring than a bus terminus with its vending machines and dubious toilets which rarely have the holy trinity of working lock, toilet paper and soap.

Airports have much more in their favour, namely the globe and bringing its most glamorous destinations all within reach. There is something energising about hanging out in a terminal with people bound for Honolulu or Tahiti even if we are bound for somewhere more mundane. Eating and shopping always features high on people's lists of favourite things to do, and airports have these pursuits well catered for.

Airports demand punctuality which might explain the myriad opportunities to purchase watches. Mostly luxury marques, bound by the same time that constrains us all, yet somehow for a whacking premium.

And perfumes of course, surely the greatest waste of money on

Earth, with so much shelled out for so little. Logically, a flight should be the most fragrant place we ever encounter since half the passengers have just emptied testers all over themselves. And yet we can't smell anything on a flight which is proof that our money is better spent elsewhere.

Airports offer glamour too with the chance to stargaze. Celebrities I mean. Our own entrance into an arrival's hall is our fleeting moment in the spotlight with the excited waiting hoards and all eyes upon us.

Airport reunions are common and lovely to observe. I like to estimate how long the separation has been judging by the tears, hugs and cheers. Some people bring banners and balloons which they probably regret at some point – when disposing of them at least?

Reunions are usually joyous occasions. The time I flew to Thailand to surprise Sam and Harry for their birthday and coinciding with Tom's wrap party for the filming of *The Impossible*. Maybe I was worried it might be his last such wrap party?

But reunions can also be sad occasions which brings me to a cold Monday morning at Heathrow Airport where I was meeting one of my oldest friends off a flight from Australia. His trip had been hastily arranged and made much more complicated by Covid. He was scheduled to land at 7 a.m. and I would be there waiting for him – but then he called with news that his flight had been brought forward. Now with a new 5 a.m. arrival (stupid o'clock), he kindly stood me down for a taxi instead and immediately I spied an opportunity for a happy surprise. Happy for me to see him and presumably for him also with his taxi fare saved.

Bleary eyed, I waited in the hall, my excitement building but also my sense of sadness.

Some men have loads of friends. Typically, those who played team sports or company men with years at the same firm. Or just organised types who have the energy and ability to keep in touch and can be bothered to do so.

I am none of the above. Nikki organises my life. Holidays, dinners outs, weekends…

In fact, the only thing I am solely responsible for is my job. Being funny in the right place, at the correct time and for the agreed number of minutes in order to get paid.

As such, there are lots of people in my life I am fond of and friendly with, but I have few very close friends and these all extend back to my inglorious school days. Four lads in particular; our bond being stronger for the formative life landmarks we experienced together.

Which is why I was excited at Heathrow but also desperately sad. Because my mate had made the longest journey possible – Sydney to London – to attend the funeral of our close buddy who we had known for over forty years.

The four are now three.

A happy airport reunion for two old school chums but underpinned by hurt. We were set to meet with our third pal for a nice week ahead. Drinking and reminiscing in the London pubs that we frequented back in the day as a four and then we waved him off with our prayers, hopes and unanswered questions. A lovely guy whom we all loved very much and are despondent to lose far too soon.

RIP

Michael Tapia

22.09.65 – 12.11.21

Michael has a strong hand in this book since it was he who encouraged me to begin writing my blog. My first blog posts were at his insistence not to mention his technical know-how. This book is a direct outcome of my blog and why it feels fitting to include this Take and a poignant way to sign off.

Epilogue

Well, having finished this volume, the burning question now might be…

How do you feel?

Do you feel good? Or at least, do you feel better than you did when you started reading?

Too strong? Too soon? Too needy?

But thank you for finishing. You might be an avid reader and have polished it off quickly. Or it might be the first book you have completed in a long time. I hope this feels like an achievement and on this I share a further anecdote…

A while ago, I was hosting a boozy dinner at a posh hotel. A tough looking bloke approached me with a quizzical look on his reddened and pinched face. He started asking me questions about whether I might have written a novel he had read…

Quickly we established that I was indeed the author and his face lit up.

"D'you know what? That's the only book I've ever read. I was chuffed. I f**** loved it. Made me cry, you c***."

High praise indeed and a heartening exchange. We shook hands warmly and on the matter of enjoying *Takes on Life, Vol.2*, you will know whether I overreached in the prologue.

I hope you chuckled at least at my sexual health scare or my maths debacle and that you paused at any sage moments herein. If so, I am grateful to anyone willing to write a review for this book on *Amazon, Good Reads* and elsewhere but I suggest without the vernacular of our aforementioned reviewer.

Takes on Life is accompanied by my podcast with the same title. Each episode is framed by an individual *Take* from volumes 1 or 2, followed by a discussion and chat with a guest. The podcast is free on various audio channels but for a fuller fix, you can join me on Patreon to watch full episodes plus further video discussions with readers, writing tutorials and much else besides.

My blog continues each Sunday on **www.dominicholland.co.uk**

And for those interested…

The novel referred to above which made a grown man cry, is *Open Links*. And this is not a craven plug by a grasping author, since ALL proceeds from *Open Links* are paid to *Anthony Nolan*, a charity that saves hundreds of lives every year from blood cancer and I feel is a fitting way to end this 'important' book by offering us all a highly valuable and useful sense of perspective.

Lightning Source UK Ltd.
Milton Keynes UK
UKHW042107310123
416258UK00001B/1

9 781739 786045